My Dear Father
Gurdjieff

My Dear Father
Gurdjieff

Nikolai de Stjernvall

Bardic Press

2013

First English edition copyright © 2013 Bardic Press.

All rights reserved.

ISBN: 978-1-906834-01-2

An English translation of the French title *Daddy Gurdjieff* by Nicolas de Val, originally issued in 1997 by publisher Georg. Although Nikolai de Stjernvall preferred using his actual name, his work was released under a pen name at Georg's insistence.

Credits:

Primary texts by Nikolai de Stjernvall.

"Across the Caucasus with G. I. Gurdjieff" and "Meetings with Rasputin" by Elizaveta de Stjernvall.

"The Last Days of Katherine Mansfield" by Adele Kafian.

Translation, "Foreword" and "About the Author" by Paul Beekman Taylor.

Dust jacket photograph by Toni von Horn reproduced with the kind permission of Charles van Horne. Depicted are (left to right above) Louise Goepfert and Jeanne de Salzmann, (below) Gurdjieff, Nikolai de Stjernvall and Dr Leonid de Stjernvall, and (in front) Michel de Salzmann.

Editing and design by L. S. Negrin.

Bardic Press
71 Kenilworth Park
Dublin 6W
Ireland

On the occasion of the publication of my recollections of Gurdjieff, I would like to thank for their collaboration Yona Birker Chavanne, Christopher Stegman, Paul B. Taylor, Roland Talmatchoff and a long-time friend who wishes to remain unnamed who has recently died. May his soul rest in peace!

Nikolai de Stjernvall
June 1997

CONTENTS

Foreword	*i*
About the Author	*v*
Introduction	*1*
Le Prieuré des Basses Loges	*9*
Gurdjieff and Normandy	*29*
Paris	*35*
Other Memories	*53*
Across the Caucuses with G. I. Gurdjieff	*55*
In Place of a Conclusion	*81*
My Mother and Her Wish to Have a Child	*83*
The Last Days of Katherine Mansfield	*91*
Notes	*99*
Photographs	*101*

FOREWORD

Georgivanich Gurdjieff, reviewing in November 1927 the finished draft of the first series of his writing, entitled *Beelzebub's Tales to His Grandson,* came to a realization that 'The form of the exposition of my thoughts in these writings could be understood exclusively by those readers who, in one way or another, were already acquainted with the peculiar form of my mentation... But every other reader... would understand nearly nothing' (*Life Is Real,* p. 5). This caveat has continued to hold true for those who did know Gurdjieff personally, or could not grasp an appreciable sense of the man in his writings. Since Gurdjieff's death in 1949, there has been an enormous amount written about his ideas, and now those ideas have been diluted by their application to the mainstream of 'New Age' thought. Too little has been written, however, about the man himself, for it remains that, without sensing the human vitality of the author, it is difficult, if not impossible to grasp the essence of his work.

Besides James Moore's magisterial Gurdjieff biography published in 1991, there are but scattered and brief sketches of Gurdjieff, and none have been able to detail the intimate quotidian life of Gurdjieff. Nikolai de Stjernvall shared and observed every facet of that life. First, as a young boy at the Prieuré, he was one of the oldest of a large group of children; and then, as a young man, he lived with Gurdjieff in a crowded apartment in Paris where he fulfilled the role of Gurdjieff's major domo, a man for all seasons in every aspect of the master's domestic life. In this capacity, Nikolai de Stjernvall had a unique occasion to take note of the very human side of a man revered as exotic, fantastic and extraordinarily superhuman by many who ignore his humanity beneath his mask as trickster.

Gurdjieff's trickster powers are most evident in the story of his extraordinary escape with a large entourage in 1919 from the Russian Revolution. That exodus began in an area in the Caucasus where Nikolai de Stjernvall was born himself in September 1919. The only other record we have of this amazing trek, besides Gurdjieff's own casual remarks in the coda to *Meetings with Remarkable Men,* is the account of Thomas de Hartmann, Nikolai's godfather. Those memoirs added to these of Nikolai's mother, Elizaveta de Stjernvall, are of inestimable value in displaying the wonderful scope of Gurdjieff's practical genius. Some years later at the Prieuré, this practical artistry, which some would call 'magic', was paramount for the large number of children about him. He cherished the very young, and he directed their activities with particular care for their future development. One aspect of that care is illustrated in Nikolai's recollection of Gurdjieff's frequent call *pomni sebia,* a command whose literal sense—'remember oneself'—can convey little of its broad and profound sense.

Gurdjieff both guided and tested those he loved constantly, and his tests took many forms from simple tasks in isolation to participation in what may seem like frightening demonstrations of his own skills, among many, as a driver, tradesman, and cook. Gurdjieff was a keen observer of others and an exacting judge of their performances as well as of his own. Though many children forgot in time their privileged lessons, Nikolai did not, and the following record offers the reader a vivid portrait of a man who welcomed and cultivated every aspect of his full and challenging life.

I was with both Nikolai and Gurdjieff briefly at the Prieuré in the early 1930s, but was too young to hold in my memory more than a few vague images of games on the lawn and odours in the kitchen. My mother took me to visit Nikolai and his parents later in Normandy, of which my only recollection is of a bicycle I wanted to be able to ride. I met Nikolai again in Geneva in 1949—when I was with Gurdjieff as a sort of mechanic and handyman—and I have profited from his company here in Geneva for the past few years. This is just to say that I knew Gurdjieff long ago and know Nikolai well enough now to appreciate that this memoir rings true to its author and its subject.

Paul B. Taylor
Geneva, January 1997

ABOUT THE AUTHOR

Nikolai de Stjernvall was born in Tbilisi on 28th September 1919 to Elizaveta Grigorievna de Stjernvall and Leonid Robertovich de Stjernvall, both born in Russian Finland. Though his biological father was Georgivanich Gurdjieff, Leonid, who was several years older than his wife and unable to give her a child, was overjoyed with the birth of a son to his wife. Nikolai was born only a few months after his parents had completed their hazardous journey with Gurdjieff across the Caucasus.

In July 1920, nine months after his birth, Nikolai and his parents left Russia by boat with Gurdjieff for Constantinople, and a year later by train they accompanied Gurdjieff to Berlin. In July 1922 they accompanied Gurdjieff to Paris and a few weeks later they moved with the entire Gurdjieff entourage to the Prieuré (Priory) in Avon, a suburb of Fontainebleau. Nikolai spent the next ten years there in the company of countless other children, to many of whom he was related by blood. Along with most of the other children of the Prieuré, he attended local schools in Fontainebleau, learning French, though he continued to speak Russian at home with his parents and the other children at the Prieuré.

He was thirteen years old when, after Gurdjieff closed his Institute for the Harmonious Development of Man in late 1932, he moved with his family to a village near Rouen in Normandy, where he completed his schooling. When he was eighteen, Gurdjieff called him to his apartment on the Rue des Colonels Renard to serve as a domestic aid, what Nikolai called appropriately, a 'factotum'. He returned to

Normandy in 1938 just before Leonid de Stjernvall died of prostate cancer. When the Second World War broke out in September 1939, he and his mother boarded a ship for Stockholm, and from there to Helsinki. After settling in Helsinki, Nikolai, just barely twenty years of age, Finnish by birth, joined the armed forces in a war defending against the invading Soviet army. Having learned Finnish, and fluent in French and Russian, he was assigned intelligence tasks in a department attached to Field Marshal Carl Gustav Emil Mannerheim. At the war's end, he translated for Mannerheim documents into French and, although his mother wanted to return to France, Mannerheim, who was about to leave for Switzerland for medical treatment, helped Nikolai find work as an interpreter for the United Nations in Geneva. In 1948 he and his mother settled in Geneva. Nikolai remained there with his mother until her death. He never married.

Nikolai, like his half-brother Michel de Salzmann, resembled Gurdjieff physically. Unlike Michel he did not follow Gurdjieff's teachings after the death of his father. Since Michel, a psychiatrist, had a practise in Geneva, and directed a Gurdjieff group there, the two saw each other often. After he retired from freelance interpreting, Nikolai travelled to Canada, England and the United States to visit relatives and close friends such as Boris Mouravieff, Dushka Howarth, and Lida and Luba Gurdjieff. In 1996 Nikolai suffered a stroke, but never lost his mental powers. In 2007 he moved to a retirement home in Veyrier, outside Geneva, where he remained until his death 26th June 2010.

Despite his zest for life, food, drink and the company of others, Nikolai was a lonely man, and his remembrance of his biological father grew in importance during his years alone. His cherished image of Gurdjieff, highlighted with modesty in his closing salute to his "dear father," is conveyed subtly but surely.

INTRODUCTION

Numerous works, more or less serious, have been published to date on Georgivanich Gurdjieff, his origins, his many tribulations and his first appearances in Moscow, Saint Petersburg and other places in Russia before and during the October Revolution in 1917. His teaching has also been amply documented and commented upon, as well as the personalities of certain of his many disciples. Thus it goes without saying that I will abstain from repeating the same facts and opinions which have already been pronounced and echoed concerning Monsieur Gurdjieff.[1] My objective is quite simple, without ambition or literary pretension.

My god-father Thomas de Hartmann recalls appropriately in his reminiscences entitled *Our Life with Mr Gurdjieff*—and I cite him freely from memory—'if what I have to say is not written now, it will be lost forever.' I must admit that I feel the same urgency, and the view back in time is in my case considerably further. Having arrived at the twilight of my life, it seems to me to be the proper time to reconstitute the distant past, my boyhood at the Prieuré des Basses Loges, meetings with people, impressions, some episodes experienced which have not yet been disclosed, anecdotes, and so forth, all associated with the person of Gurdjieff. My purpose ends there. It is a matter, after all, of a new testimony on my part, without ostentation or presumption, which will add value to all those testimonies already in the public eye.

I judge it not too late to share with others who have known G.I., and who have up until now honoured his memory, the few recollections which I retain and which ask no more than to be recounted. On the other hand, that which sets me apart from the number of authors who have preceded me, is that many of them neither knew nor met G.I. personally. For this occasion, then, I can allow myself certain liberties, since I will speak of my progenitor, a fact not negligible in this context. I have, unfortunately, lost sight of my half-brothers and -sisters, whom I abstain from naming but who are quite numerous, dispersed as they are at present throughout the world.

༄

I had seen Georgivanich Gurdjieff in Paris in 1939 just before the Second World War. The five years I had to spend in the Finnish army between 1939 and 1944 because of my legal nationality, prevented me, of course, from pursuing university studies, and even less from learning a trade. I had many responsibilities to assume in the army, certain of which are of a confidential character. During the war I encountered real dangers, deprivations, sorrow and, at times, the rigours of the front line. My mother, who chose to follow me to Finland for as long as I served under the flag in combat, spoke to me frequently of an eventual return to France after the torment of war. It was, finally, in Switzerland, in Geneva, where we ended up in November 1948 after a long voyage by train across a Germany devastated by allied bombardments. We got off the train in Geneva, a bit like itinerant players, with our kitchenware and our meagre goods, all divided up into sixteen packages. The first months in Geneva were exceptionally hard on us, and we were forced to scrape by as best we could.

Jeanne de Salzmann, one of Gurdjieff's first disciples, his uncontested right hand, intimate confidante and guardian of his teaching, had never broken contact with us since 1939. This incomparable woman who had been witness, so to speak, of my birth in the Caucasus during our exodus from Russia, kept us up to date regularly of whatever events taking place in France might interest us. I wish to render homage here to Jeanne de Salzmann, who never left us in adversity and whose bounty for our sake was beyond measure. It was she who announced to us the probable arrival of Gurdjieff in Geneva in July 1949.

༄

For a considerable amount of time my mother and I waited aimlessly on the sidewalk in front of the Hotel Bristol on the Rue du Mont-Blanc in Geneva. The anticipated caravan of cars finally came into sight, Gurdjieff's 15-horsepower Citroën in the lead, followed by two large automobiles which lined up, more or less in order, along the sidewalk near the hotel. A pale smile lit up Georgivanich's face when he noticed my mother and me on the street. Never any show of emotions or embraces with the master! It was as if we had seen him the night before.

I hurried to the Citroën to help Gurdjieff out of his car. I was surprised to see him, head covered with a fez, oriental leather slippers on his feet, and without glasses at his age! He supported himself on my shoulder and took considerable pains to pull himself out of the car. I found him very tired, extremely aged and worn. His face had the colour of earthen clay. Heavy bags under his eyes hid what was once a piercing look. He shook my hand softly and gave my mother a salute with a nod of his head. The features on the face of G. I. seemed frozen to me.

While we were standing on the sidewalk, Georgivanich asked me to go buy a pack of Celtiques as well as Sobranie— luxurious cigarettes generally difficult to find—but they were available at the Rhein tobacco shop across the street from the hotel. He watched me cross the street to make my purchase, and when I returned, he exclaimed in Russian:

'Look at that! What is this hasnamuss[2] swing of the hips! You had better watch the way you walk!'

He had to make everyone aware that the acuity of his vision and his sense of observation were intact!

I did not know who all the people were in his entourage. There were many unfamiliar faces at first view. Besides, the greater part of those who were with G.I. dispersed almost immediately. I learned later that Georgivanich had been held up for some time at the Swiss border because he did not have all the documents the Swiss customs demanded. Two very attractive young girls left the group to join us, each carrying an elegant valise full of exotic drinks, foods and sweets.

Gurdjieff, my mother, Jeanne de Salzmann, Dorothy Caruso (the widow of the famous Italian tenor), and myself, as well as two others who were strangers to me, went together into a small salon in the Hotel Bristol. It was obvious that the location was far from pleasing to G.I. He exploded instantly, but a bit softly as far as I was concerned compared to the explosions of his anger and his notorious shouts in public in the old days.

'I can't stay in this miserable place.' he yelled. Then addressing Jeanne de Salzmann: 'Find me something else right away, Jeanne!'

I saw poor Jeanne cross the Rue du Mont-Blanc and head toward the Hotel des Bergues, well-known in Geneva. She came back a half hour later with good news. There was room for Georgivanich on the other side of Rue du Mont Blanc at the Hotel de la Paix, facing the lake.

I would not go so far as to say that Gurdjieff came all the way to Geneva just see my mother and me; but, at any rate, he was not ignorant of our presence in this city and of our long separation. While Jeanne was away in search of another hotel, Gurdjieff made a sign to the young girls who had joined us in the little salon of the Bristol. To my great joy I saw one of them coming up to my mother with an envelope in her hand. The second girl, who was sitting next to me, handed me an unsealed envelope. A quick glance revealed that a number of dollar notes, which, considering the exchange rates at the time (4.37 Swiss francs to the dollar), was manna from heaven for us. Once again, the incredible intuition and incomparable goodness of Georgivanich's heart showed itself in a remarkable gesture. God knows that this money arrived in the nick of time. The smile which spread across my mother's face at the moment she opened her own envelope could not fool anyone.

'Come and see me at the hotel before dinner,' G. I. said abruptly.

'You must also see to a greasing and oil change for the car.'

Curiously, it was almost always the same scenario; that is to say that perhaps for the thirtieth time, as soon as we met, Georgivanich would put me in charge of checking the oil and having a grease job done for his car. When late that afternoon I knocked on the door of Gurdjieff's room at the Hôtel de la Paix, I found him sitting on the bidet, his face in pain, suffering again from his swollen stomach and his almost chronic gas accumulations. Despite the medications he took regularly, he would not give up carbonated mineral water, alcohol and spicy foods. He was never ill at ease in front of me, no matter his discomfort. I watched him undress quickly and found it difficult to suppress my feelings before such an ill man, literally at the end of his tether. To see him like that in his long underwear, relaxed for a moment, reminded me immediately of the period I had served him as his factotum in Paris in 1937.

I felt suddenly at ease. The atmosphere in this hotel room seemed familiar and intimate to me.

'Pass me my trousers,' he said abruptly. I saw him take

some large Swiss banknotes out of a dark wallet, which he handed to me with an unforgettable gentleness. 'Take care of the car. I'm expecting both of you for dinner,' he added.

We all gathered together at the first-class buffet at the Cornavin railway station in Geneva. As I have already remarked, a number of people present at that dinner were strangers to me. Dorothy Caruso held the purse strings. I have forgotten somewhat the numerous rituals which one had to observe in the company of Georgivanich. To my deep regret, the master remained practically silent throughout the entire meal. The orchestra, which played rather loudly, had a gift for irritating Gurdjieff. The maître d'hôtel was called for on the spot, and a large tip (for the times) was offered him with an order to quiet the musicians or to have them put on the dampers. Although I cannot recall the exact reaction of the other diners in the room, I am left with the impression that they were hardly able to control their curiosity toward our conspicuous table.

There was, of course, in the first place, the personality of G.I., his outward appearance, but also the glasses of armagnac, peppered vodka, smoked bear and camel meat which made the rounds. Gurdjieff surprised me considerably when he broke his silence to me: 'Why did you leave France in 1939? You could have been a general by now, you silly ass!' Then, turning to Jeanne de Salzmann: 'There must surely be a Citroën agent in this city. I insist that Kolia have his own car as well. Go look.'

One can imagine that this was a promise which filled me with pleasure. Jeanne de Salzmann acquitted herself perfectly with the task that G.I. has charged her in front of everyone, even if the promised automobile was only a very comfortable Austin. I might add that this entire exchange took place in Russian, to the discomfort of the others at the table. Gurdjieff seemed very tired and was obviously eager to start back for Paris as soon as possible. He made an appointment to see my mother and myself the following morning. On my side, I was concerned with his Citroën. The next morning along the sidewalk by the hotel I parked an automobile meticulously greased, oiled and washed. Georgivanich was not in good form and kept silent. A small part of the group was still in the café. The other two large automobiles and their occupants waited not far from the Citroën. Meanwhile, my mother appeared at the café. As was his habit, G.I. served himself black coffee with a lemon ring and a small bottle of Perrier. My mother and I were sitting very close to him. He spoke to us suddenly in a rapid burst of Russian. 'The strong boxes in Swiss banks are bursting under the weight of my money.' That was about all he felt it proper to tell us before leaving.

I looked continuously at a face showing extreme fatigue. He had lost completely his usual vivacity and conviviality. He got up with difficulty and I went with him to his Citroën. My mother thanked him with affection for his generosity and wished him well for his return home. Switching on the starter, Georgivanich gave us a final and enigmatic look, half-sad, half-affectionate. He waved weakly and disappeared soon in the flow of traffc, followed by his escort. That was the last image of G.I. which I hold in my memory. As everyone knows, Georgivanich Gurdjieff died at the American Hospital in Neuilly, Paris, on 29th October 1949.

₪

LE PRIEURÉ DES BASSES LOGES
Rue de Valvins, Avon (Seine et Marne)

To evoke a time long past in a coherent fashion when one has one foot in the grave is hardly easy for one who arrived at the Prieuré at the age of three and a half. This vast domain had belonged previously to Fernand Labori, the defending attorney of Captain Dreyfus. The widow of the lawyer sold the furnished building to Gurdjieff. Thanks to funds gathered with great difficulty, the domain's many annexes were also acquired. Things being as they were, so to say, I must go back in time and put some chronological order to my narrative.

The Prieuré, or more precisely the Institute for the Harmonious Development of Man, represented for its adult residents an uninterrupted and tormenting physical and intellectual labour, often without reward. As things were, there were no privileged persons at the Prieuré, with the exception of some older English ladies in failing health, and a few important guests and personalities passing through. Daily life was hard for most of them, especially so for the few who then gravitated around Gurdjieff, accepted his teaching, and submitted themselves willingly to the rigours and constraints of its methods.

Schematically, the teaching was conceived as follows:

The civilisation of our day, with its infinite possibilities, has progressively distanced modern man from his initial structure. It has deprived him of the normal conditions under which he could have lived. It has pushed him toward new and sterile aspirations. In a word, it has prevented his harmonious development. Our psychic body does not constitute a unique and indivisible wholeness. It consists, to the contrary, of three distinct interior entities which do not collaborate together. More exactly, Gurdjieff identifies these three centres as the thinking, emotional and motor centres.

Man's willed perceptions and manifestations are, therefore, the result of the concomitant action of these three centres. One can affirm, for this reason, that three different beings live in each of us: a logical, an emotional and an automatic being. In our actions, each of the three beings which live in us manifest its respective weight and become known as me. If, then, we aspire to a true psychic equilibrium in coherent thought and act, we have to assure ourselves of a better coordination of our three centres. Man is born to be omniscient. To know how to do everything, act with confidence, master his weaknesses, develop his mental faculties and his body, know nature and himself: these are, in brief, the necessary conditions for harmonious development.

∽

We lived in the Paradou, one of the charming annexes of the Prieuré. At that time the children there were watched over in turn by the various mothers. It was a routine that G.I. had instituted so that the young ones would not get used to being spoiled by their own mothers. Gurdjieff considered also that children had to grow up, broaden in scope and develop harmoniously like plants, which, à priori, excluded traditional schooling, the acquisition of theoretical knowledge or other restraints of the spirit. I remember, a bit confusedly, it is true, Katherine Mansfield, her frail silhouette, her short dark hair and her very personal smile. Katherine taught us the rudiments of drawing. The little group of pupils included at the time 'Boussique' (Natalie, the daughter of Jeanne de Salzmann), Yvonne Pinder, Lonia, the grandson of Madame Ouspensky, and myself.

To this softly stamped recollection is attached, unfortunately, that of a vicious hag named Ethel Merston, an old maid full of herself and ugly as a spider. For the least thing this creature punished us—Boussique and me—tying us to trees as the Sioux did to their captives. Another time, we deserved a little spanking, administered by Alexander de Salzmann after he caught me playing doctor in the orangery, examining conscientiously my little undressed friend. Everywhere at the Prieuré one saw frescos and paintings, drawings and other works of art which adorned the walls and ceilings of the Institute. There were also inscriptions of the memento-mori type. All these works were done by the talented Alexander de Salzmann, who had completed his studies at the Academy of Fine Arts at Munich. I can still see this exceptional artist carrying buckets, palettes and large paint brushes. It took him but a few minutes to bring to life on the walls fields or woods filled with deer, hare, squirrels, various birds, etc. Alexander de Salzmann surpassed himself in decorating superbly the small balcony-like platform with staircase which was fixed up in the cowshed where Katherine Mansfield spent many hours every day, since the air of the place was thought salutary for her lungs infected by tuberculosis.

Here I abstain intentionally from evoking the death of Katherine Mansfield whose husband John Middleton Murry arrived just before her last day. Much has already been written about that, and Adele Kafian's unpublished testimony is appended as an annex to my memoir.

Adele, a Lithuanian who spoke impeccable Russian, had been attached to the service of Katherine and had cared for her to her last breath. Adele's husband, an Armenian mathematician, was called Christopher, or Christi. I had the pleasure of meeting both of them again in Paris a long time afterwards. Adele was not only a poetess, decorator and writer in her time, but she was an admirable painter. She was given the job, among others, of copying certain tapestries of Alexander de Salzmann, copies almost impossible to distinguish form the originals.

The children adored the end of the year festivities and especially the sight of the traditional Christmas tree, superbly decorated, which was set up always in the grand salon of the Prieuré. With hearts beating, we unwrapped the large white hat boxes filled with all kinds of presents which the adults in our community had collected for us. Seated in his usual place, G.I., with an affectionate smile on his face, liked to observe our reactions and obviously shared our pleasure.

I remember well the mother of Georgivanich. She was a simple woman, often dressed in black with a lace on her head. She seemed to me someone without anything to do, and she liked to cite Armenian sayings all the time. G.I. treated her with respect, but no more. I remember also, despite my tender years, Julia, Gurdjieff's wife, thin and lithe, who died unfortunately in the flower of her age, wracked by tuberculosis.

There was also Dmitri, known also as 'Mido', the younger brother of Georgivanich, for whom he showed genuine affection, as well as a great deal of indulgence! Mido was a sybarite, gambler, lover of idle banter in the public rooms of Fontainebleau where he liked to spend his time. Mido and his wife Asta had three daughters, Luba, Genia and Lida. One time, when Genia and I were near the garage in a sort of courtyard, her father, who was passing by, without any apparent reason, and with an evil grin on his face, broke a dry branch over her calves. Poor Genia! The unloved one, while her sister Lida—or Lidiko—remained Mido's pet. I liked the wife of Georges Lvovich Kapanadze, G.I.'s sister Sophie, who always had a slightly sad smile on her face. Valentin, another nephew a bit older than I, strong as a Turk, with a manly profile, and Lucia, also one of Gurdjieff's nieces, a hard worker, warm and modest, filled out the family, or 'clan'.

All of these relatives gravitated about Georgivanich and lived permanently at the Prieuré, where they performed various tasks. But, there were also a number of other residents, such as Bernard Metz, a sensitive type and a constant grouch, Tchesslav Tchekhovitch, Olga Vachadze, Payson Loomis, Rachmielevitch, Schuyler Jackson, Peggy Mathews, Jane Heap, Miss Gordon, Miss Alexander, Miss Potter, Louise Goepfert, etc. To this group I might add a few 'anonymous' persons who had no precise functions to fulfil and who made themselves useful as best they could. Edith Taylor, one among others, with a somewhat austere air, lived also at the Prieuré. She fascinated me a lot. She owned a superb Delage convertible with an elegant interior of light-coloured leather impregnated with the perfume of its owner. Whenever I could I found the chance to get into the car secretly and to dream languidly at length, taking pleasure in the multiple stimulating odours it gave off.

Thomas de Hartmann, alias 'Foma' as G.I. called him, was an exceptional musician, a master of harmony. He played perfectly Gurdjieff's musical compositions. I often saw him at his grand piano listening to G.I. whistle oriental airs and other tunes, while in a frenzy he would be jotting down their musical notes. Thomas, my god-father, discovered that I had absolute pitch and a good sense of rhythm. Others told me that I performed easily the rhythmical movements, could freeze perfectly in the game of 'stop', and possessed the necessary suppleness for the exercises.

Jeanne de Salzmann, Olga Vachadze, Lili Galumnian and Nina Mercurov, among others, including many men, were experienced at the dances and movements taught by

Gurdjieff. This spectacle usually took place in the 'Study House', an old aeroplane hangar transformed into a temple by the disciples. There was also Foma's wife, who lived at the Prieuré with her parents, the Schumachers. My little boy's eyes followed closely the activities of this entire world of adults. Every day I saw men and women careless of their dress, working hard, their backs hunched. Some pushed wheelbarrows, some dug trenches, others spaded the earth, raked paths, split wood, made repairs, tended equipment, etc. Intellectuals and white-collar types were in it at their peril.

My own mother, coming from a comfortable middle class, had to learn to milk the community's cows under assignment for a certain period which obliged her to rise in the wee hours, but which she accomplished conscientiously. Georgivanich occasionally held inspection upon arriving on the spot without warning, observing workers for a while, giving instructions or showing how to do something with gestures surprisingly precise and sure. I repeat that the children were lucky. Lonia, Boussique, Yvonne, Michel de Salzmann, Tom and Fritz Peters, somewhat older than the rest, as well as G.I.'s nieces, were my playmates. Besides the dogs Philos, Black and Mramor, we liked all the other animals at the Prieuré.

In this context, I have always held a grudge against Patchuli, a real s.o.b., a Caucasian sort of jack-of-all-trades who lived at the Institute. One day when I was passing in front of a temporary stable, I spotted Dralfit, our quiet and gentle mule, lying on the ground. The poor animal had caught pneumonia and could not even get up. It was then that I saw Patchuli armed with a club, with which he started to beat the mule savagely on the head. I still remember the agony of poor Dralfit.

Some time later, Gurdjieff's disciples were ordered to put together a real stable for three cows and a box for Fifi, a nice black mare. I rode Fifi bareback, but put on her a rude bridle before leading her out of the stable, picking my time judiciously. Then I would gallop her across the underbrush and the park at the Prieuré. One day, during one of these wild rides, I had the misfortune of slipping with my mount into a rather deep ravine which G.I.'s disciples had dug around the bath-house, itself set into an enormous excavation. I had to get Fifi out as quickly as possible from this damn mud hole. The entry to this ravine was through a trench covered with planks which served as a provisional path. It was only after taking up the planks one by one and putting them in place side-by-side that I was able to make a passage from the trench and gain freedom.

One bright day Gurdjieff made a present of a superb electric car to Michel. Such toys, equipped with steering and powered by a very special motor, were still rare and expensive at this time. In order not to cause jealousy among the other children, G.I. decided to offer me a donkey, Marishka, with her colt who answered to the name Friquette. Races across the domain of the Prieuré were veritable delights. As all burros, Marishka, a model of her kind, was stubborn and resisted direction. I realised that to mount her I had to equip myself with a big stick and even use spurs. We went as far as to buy a harness, a saddle and even a cart for my outings in town. It was precisely during one of these outings in Fontainebleau with Papoussia[3] that I recount here briefly. Papoussia held the reins and everything was going without problem until the outskirts of the town when, suddenly, Marishka stopped short and lay on the tram tracks. Despite the traffic backup which took place, the angry blows and yelling of the tram conductor, nothing would budge Marishka. Finally one of the onlookers told us to go look for the butcher in the neighbourhood who had, we were told, an infallible method for reasoning with the stubborn. I ran, then, to ask for the butcher's help, who arrived in haste on the scene with a pair of tongs in his hand. It was easy to guess the kind of operation the man was about to perform. In fact, he went ahead with his exploration of Marishka's jaw, and pushed the tongs into her mouth energetically, Realizing the treatment which was about to follow, Marishka got up with a jolt, kicked up her heels and shot off in the direction of the Prieuré leaving us in place, powerless and completely taken aback! I restrain from recounting other episodes of this sort, but there were many.

As I have already indicated, Gurdjieff had his ideas on religion, cult practises, children's schooling, etc. At the Prieuré, in the fiefdom where he reigned as absolute master, he could do what he wished. Besides cries and yells of all sorts, he fell occasionally into states of megalomania, in the style of 'Me God, me God medicine, science, physical,' etc. These excesses were often blasphemous oaths against beliefs or religious convictions of someone or other. Yet I had the impression often that he did not take himself seriously in such outcries. Appropriately, mostly because of his linguistic handicap, Gurdjieff surrounded himself with competent, intelligent and cultivated people. Nevertheless, it must be admitted that practically no one dared defy, contradict, criticize or lead him into an argument, or even react to the humiliations which he forced occasionally his disciples to bear. The only one who could hold his head high by saying to his face, in Armenian, what he thought of him was his own brother Mido, because G.I. had taken it upon himself to become a part of the household and the private life of his younger brother. At the end of violent confrontations between the two, the master could be seen leaving ashamed for having been opposed.

Gurdjieff obviously had a personality out of the ordinary. The mastery which he exercised over his adepts was almost limitless. More or less everyone was subjugated to his will. Some admired G.I., some venerated him, while others openly hated him. His occult powers, the aura of mystery which surrounded him, his magnetic personality, his extraordinary intuition, were such that women of all rank and social standing could not resist him and succumbed to his charm, so much so that his detractors did not hesitate to qualify him as demonic. As far as my mother is concerned, she had but one desire, to have a child. On top of that, a son had been predicted for her by Rasputin, whom she had had the occasion to know in Saint Petersburg long before she met G.I. Rasputin's prophecy was thus realized. It was hardly for me to judge, to criticize or to ask questions about my mother's acts and decisions. I can only add that I was conceived in the Caucasus on board a ship between 5:00 and 6:00 PM.

ಲ

Readings from *Beelzebub* took place usually in the grand salon or the drawing room just under the luxury rooms of the 'Ritz'. Disciples who attended these reading sessions gathered around Georgivanich, often after a strenuous day of all sort of physical activities. Most of them kept their eyes lowered as they listened religiously in absolute silence to Gurdjieffian prose. The texts, which were primarily Russian, were read by members of his intimate entourage chosen and trained especially for the purpose. As for G.I., he feasted on flattery. With his wide expression, bright eyes, puffing furiously without interruption on his Russian cigarettes, he laughed now and then while scrutinizing faces and noting varieties of reactions. This self-satisfaction which he displayed even before the smallest of crowds, was undeserving to his intelligence, I said to myself. Nevertheless, he had a pet dog who did not respect silence or the attention which reigned in this place. Philos, whom G.I.

had come to love, a mongrel with a trumpet tail, infested with fleas and anus encrusted with filth, and who showed up unwelcome everywhere, did not care at all. Nonchalant, sure of himself, he stretched himself out in the middle of the salon under the indulgent eyes of the audience.

☙

No one was permitted to leave the grounds of the Prieuré without a valid reason. There was no formal interdiction expressed to this effect, but it was implicit to most of the residents. Close to the main gate there was a sort of guard house where someone was usually stationed to maintain order and to carry out orders from the main house. I remember a number of Cerberuses such as Mercurov and Svechnikov, who took their turns with a huge ring of keys in their hands and who stuck their noses everywhere.

My mother, who was a very pious and fervent Christian, pretended to ignore certain rules in practise at the Prieuré such as, among others, schooling and religious observances. So I went every day to the primary school in Avon with Tolie, the son of Mercurov. As Easter neared, my mother took me regularly to the Seminary of St. Serge on the Rue de Crimée in Paris, where we paid our observances. My confessor at that time was the celebrated Father Sergei Bulgakov, who went so far as to question me about the Institute. My mother did not care whether Gurdjieff knew about this or not.

☙

Gurdjieff had a particular fondness for automobile excursions, but only with companions of his choice. Speed and his own style of driving were intoxicants for him. Sometimes we paid visits to the sister of the celebrated creator[4] of Arsène Lupin, Georgette Leblanc, who paid special attention to me, and I repaid her to the fullest. She lived in Villennes (Seine & Marne), in a lovely setting. Miss Gordon and other old friends of the Prieuré sometimes joined our party. It must be admitted that certain faithful and meritorious residents of the Institute could not count on participating in excursions like this. G.I. was an aesthete, and travelling companions, both male and female, whose physical forms were not pleasing to him, could not expect to go along. I had often the chance of finding myself among the privileged few.

Georgivanich had particular affection for certain French districts and cities such as Vichy, Nevers, Dijon, etc. Automobile trips were marked by frequent pauses, either down off the road or in picturesque sites. Thermos bottles, drinks and many other 'emergency provisions' were always at hand, and improvised picnics on these trips found general approval. Despite a first, and then a second serious car accident, G.I. loved to drive his many cars. He drove, alas, terribly. He neither had mechanical sense nor observed the rules of the road. He took little note of distances between cars. Even when I was very young, each time I was a passenger in one of his cars, I closed my eyes and braked mentally as soon as I saw him start one of his crazy daring manoeuvres on the road in defiance of any caution. After having tried several models, he finally fixed his choice on the light Citroën, the 11-, and then the 15-horsepower with front-wheel drive. This was the car he preferred to all others for the rest of his life.

For an obscure reason, G.I. had something against Catholic priests who often went about the area on bicycle. How many times have I heard him through the lowered window of his car exclaim rudely from the front seat at frocked bicyclers. One time when he shouted loudly in Russian *svoloch*—a very degrading oath signifying according to the context, trash, stupid, etc.—taken aback, astonished, one of these poor priests lost control of his bicycle and fell heavily on the pavement.

∞

The famous steam bath, whose construction required such hard physical efforts of the disciples, was set up in an enormous excavation some eight hundred metres from the Study House. The women, and then the men, went regularly every Saturday evening. There were a few dissenters who scorned this weekly ritual, one of which was Jane Heap, whom we liked despite her slightly eccentric attire, her gravel voice and her short hair. Most of the time she wore a sort of dark smoking jacket with a bow tie or a cravat. She was obviously victim of a congenital anomaly, since she refused categorically to join the men or women in the bath. As for me, I enjoyed these common ablutions and I joined the adults in the bath each Saturday.

It was Dmitri, alias Mido, G.I.'s younger brother, who was assigned the job of heating and preparing the bath. I can see him yet, wearing a cap, joyful, stationing himself near the heater door. A few metres from there was a sort of imperial stuffed couch reserved for the master. Lowered on many cushions and rolled sheets, Georgivanich broke out in laughter listening to successions of stories, generally crude and dirty, often of Jewish or Armenian origin, which certain bathers told in competition with one another. Among the best storytellers, Alexander de Salzmann comes to mind. Straight-faced without laughter, with a slightly austere look, he had no equal in telling stories and aping accents. There was also Rachmielevitch, Mercurov and Papoussia, who were remarkable in this respect. Once emptied of their store of story, they became serious in the bath and the ablutions proceeded in good fashion. G.I. spent relatively little time in the sweat-room with its numerous benches and birch branches at the disposition of those who appreciated them, necessary if one wished to open the pores and sweat out everything. On the other hand, he took long showers and enjoyed covering his body with an nauseous pomade which took away all his body hair.

Gurdjieff had a medium build. He was just over 1.66 m (5'6"). Nonetheless, he was perfectly proportioned, despite his impressive belly. Later, when I saw him flanked by huge ill-proportioned Americans, he seemed rather small in height! G.I.'s brother-in-law Georges Kapanadze, Sophie's husband, usually took part in the Saturday evening ablutions. Georgivanich had little affection for him, calling him a parasite and good for nothing. Georges Lvovich was sickly. He was a frail little man who suffered also from haemorrhoids. The bathers had no concern for him. On the contrary, they would bring a garden hose and spray Georges' buttocks with cold water, aiming especially at his anus. Jumping in distress, then lying on his back, he begged his tormenters to stop their little game, but they only laughed louder. That which had to happen arrived naturally: I can see the miserable Kapanadze grimacing with pain, holding with both hands his colon on the verge of discharging.

But the famous Saturday evening baths were generally followed by joyous festivities in the grand dining room of the principal building, with many friendly people seated around a table filled with foods. G.I. sat on his 'throne' at the head of the famous table before a suckling pig flanked by two roast muttons. Despite the bare and ill-equipped kitchens of the time, the hors d'oeuvres and other delicacies were sumptuous and abundant. The habitual ritual of toasts to the health of idiots was observed, twenty-one of them of which Gurdjieff himself was the last toasted, that is to say the unique idiot. Readers will recall without doubt that Gurdjieff had instituted a tradition at the Prieuré which consisted of drinking to the health of 'idiots'. It goes without saying that the term 'idiot' is not to be understood in its derogatory sense, or even that it carried negative connotations. Far from it.

Gurdjieff liked to designate certain people by nicknames, often borrowed from the animal and vegetable kingdoms. These nicknames were at times slightly outrageous but always amusing, and brought to notice certain dominant traits of those so-named who gathered around the master. The ritual concerning toasts to the idiots proceeded along the same lines. As an adolescent I had the list of toasts in my head, the ordinary, recalcitrant, the hopeless, etc., but I would not be able to enumerate them today because of my failing memory. During the meals, it was rare that the number of toasts exceeded the number of nine. Only once, someone told me, did they arrive at the sixteenth toast in a euphoric mood.

But, what beverage was served to drink to the health of idiots? An exquisite old Armagnac, Chateau de Larresingle. From time to time a bottle of peppered vodka appeared, or vodka with cassis leaves, or garlic vodka, or even an old bottle of Armenian Cognac. Many times I saw G.I. tear the mutton roast with his hands and toss choice morsels to guests. Children sat at another table and could understand little of what was going on beside them. Certain of us had sometimes the grand honour of being called by G.I. to eat either the cheeks or the brain of the mutton. At four and a half I swallowed easily in a single gulp a little beaker of Armagnac to the great distress of my mother. It was an initiation which no one deemed precocious. I have not become an alcoholic as a result.

The populace of the Prieuré was not composed of anchorites and teetotallers. No one there had taken vows of chastity. What could one do to sublimate a libido which became difficult to restrain? The inhabitants managed as best they could. Men and women paired off spontaneously. Potential partners looked furtively for some time before finding sought-for intimacy, sometimes in desperation but more often with ease. Myself, I lost my virginity toward the age of nine, having succumbed to the advances of one of G.I.'s nieces slightly older than I was. I have pleasant memories of our furtive and juvenile groping, as well as of my apprenticeship in the act. Despite all their efforts and ardour at work, G.I.'s adepts had to come to terms with their sexual problems.

∞

There were certain intellectuals at the Prieuré who benefited from, one could say, a status a bit more privileged. I am thinking notably of Sophie Ouspensky, who was given free rein, but whom the children bothered. Her charming daughter Lenochka had a sparkling intelligence and a winning softness; Lenochka's son Lonia was a boyhood friend. I had a good feeling for Rachmielevitch, who treated me well. He had a rare and subtle wisdom. Rachmul, as he was called familiarly, had excellent relations with my mother. He was interesting in every respect in conversation, and commented upon and explained the teaching to my mother in a balanced and simple fashion. That teaching, one must admit, was never a favourite of my mother's. Mother and Rachmul got along splendidly, except at the table. Under the pretext that his false teeth prevented him for savouring the food as it deserved, Rachmul would take them out in front of everyone and push them into his pocket. This way of acting horrified my mother to the utmost.

Rachmul, who was Jewish, but not much of a practicing Jew, did not neglect entirely his ancestral traditions. He drew me occasionally into a discrete location, live chicken in his hand, which he put to death by suspending it by the feet and then cutting around its neck lightly with a razor blade. I had pity for the poor chicken which struggled for a long time before giving up the ghost.

◊

During our exile from Russia after the Revolution, in order to keep alive the survivors who accompanied Gurdjieff, and to permit him to support financially the needs of the group, my mother, to her great regret, had to give up a precious pair of earrings of which she was very fond. She was not the only one who had to surrender some of their riches. Other women and men had also submitted to the inevitable need. G.I. put to charitable use objects of value gathered this way. One nice day at the Prieuré, Gurdjieff gave the order to translate *Beelzebub* into German, which implied, naturally, a great deal of typing. In the beginning it was Louise Goepfert who undertook the task, but it became evident very soon that alone she could never fulfil the responsibility. My mother, who had a solid command of German, put other things aside and decided to teach herself the Remington method. After a few weeks, she was perfectly capable of typing almost professionally, and thereby gave Louise much-needed help, to the great satisfaction of Georgivanich.

A few years later, when the young Fritz Peters under orders of Georgivanich went to find my mother to return her earrings to her, she exploded with joy and gratitude because it was a total surprise. The fact is that G.I. at one time had seized the occasion to buy back the famous earrings from a Turk at a high price, and was just awaiting the right moment to give them back to their owner. Thanks to her work typing German, my mother deserved a reward.

My mother and Sophie Ouspensky were very close and saw each other almost every day. They had the same patronymic and were called, respectively, Elizaveta and Sophie Grigorievna, according to Russian usage.

❧

In 1931 Gurdjieff and his close followers—that is to say, Papoussia, Louise Goepfert and Jeanne de Salzmann (with her son Michel)—left for the United States. There was some vague question as to whether my mother, Lucia, one of G. I.'s nieces, and myself would join them a bit later in New York. Several weeks passed without any news. One bright day however, a postal money order in the name of my mother arrived from America without the least explanation. Although intrigued, she was unable to grasp its source, let alone any purpose intended by the amount sent. Without hesitating a moment, my mother went to find Sophie Ouspensky to tell her of the event, asking her advice as to what to do. Sophie, a truly perspicacious detective, counselled her friend to go to a travel agent in Fontainebleau and ask what the fare was for New York from Le Havre. The amount of the money order turned out to be exactly enough for three second-class passages. The prospect of leaving for the United States excited me greatly.

A few days later, we left Le Havre on board the *Paris,* an old steamship of the French Line. At one moment in the middle of the Atlantic, we thought our days had come to an end in the midst of a violent storm. Tossed about by the uncontrolled elements, the ship creaked and groaned incessantly. I even saw a group of nuns travelling with us mount to the boat deck to pray for the Lord's intervention.

On the whole, though, life aboard the *Paris* was truly magical for me. My poor mother who could not stand the rolls of the ship stayed prostrate in her cabin, leaving me with an open field. Despite my tender age, I made friends with many passengers, especially with an American woman who was travelling with her young daughter. She was a sociable mother full of grace and freshness. It is unnecessary to add that the food on board was wonderful.

Things started to go askew a bit at the moment we arrived in the port of New York. Papoussia and Loomis had planned to meet us at the landing. Papoussia had, unfortunately, the unhappy tendency of misjudging time, which forced him often to jump onto trains already moving. The officials of the immigration service who had come aboard before our landing, had the appearance of being tough and little given to pleasantries. On top of that, we arrived in the midst of Prohibition. Our papers, obviously, did not seem to be in order to these civil servants. They even suggested that we might be sent to Ellis Island, a place many feared, where stowaways and others without proper papers, or connections, or without sufficient funds in the United States were sent. My mother, elegant and with great dignity, was not going to be intimidated so easily. At the very instant the negotiations with the American authorities seemed to be getting nowhere, and we were ready to back down, a loud voice was heard from the pier. Loomis, with a megaphone, addressed the venomous officials with a tone of authority and ordered them to let us leave the ship at once. After offering us their excuses and welcoming us to the United States, the immigration officials let us disembark, having noticed, surely, a Rolls Royce with a uniformed chauffeur at the end of the gangway.

We stayed in a 'normal' building at 204 West 59th Street which had nothing of the appearance of the skyscrapers which surrounded us. It had a splendid view on Central Park. An American drugstore was on the ground floor, with a tobacco shop tended by Greeks. The drugstore was very popular, and the principal owner, with whom I struck up a friendship, soon let me operate the cash register of the place. I was given the job of selling cigarettes, chewing gum, etc., and earned a little bit. To pay them back, and for the pleasure of the Greeks, I brought them from time to time the leftovers of the oriental specialties we had prepared upstairs. Personally, I did not turn up my nose at the roast-beef sandwiches which my friends served me while I tended the till.

Often I joined Gurdjieff and Papoussia at Child's on Columbus Circle. At that period there were not many bearded men in the United States, and so Gurdjieff and his devoted collaborator were easily distinguished from other clients. Faithful to his habit, G.I. inked pages and pages of schoolboy notebooks with his big scrawl. It is probably worthwhile recounting briefly the mastery with which Papoussia, as moved by his inspiration and with a sleight of hand, put into acceptable form the prose which Georgivanich handed over to him in rapid succession. Tense to an extreme, smoking incessantly, G.I. watched Papoussia patiently as he corrected severely the original, which disappeared literally under innumerable crossings out. 'Where are we going with this, Doctor? Come on, come on, finish up this text, good God!' So Papoussia went to work on a veritable literary juggling act. It was a tight-rope act on the high wire. The awkward locutions and interminable and confused phrases underwent a magical remaking without losing a jot of their original sense. 'This is exactly what I wanted to say', Gurdjieff cried out, his face relaxing into joy. 'This is good, it's excellent, bravo Doctor!'

Gurdjieff himself had suggested in New York that the old 'Orage Group' should be called from now on the 'new esoteric New York group'. I have not had the courage to translate the text of the first meeting. It is available in the author's works, but only in Russian. Meetings, lectures and workshops were in full swing in the building and continued at a frantic pace. Often people had to be turned away at the door. One evening, nonetheless, G.I. was waiting for a group of disciples of whom he particularly approved. They arrived without any warning with many of their friends. The meeting lasted a long time and it was decided to serve refreshments and some sandwiches to the guests. Once again, my mother distinguished herself in practical matters by her sense of improvisation and her ability to manage under the circumstances. Under the wondering eye of Jeanne de Salzmann and Louise Goepfert, in less than half and hour, with the help of Lucia, from leftovers and some odds and ends, she put together a little buffet to the great joy of Gurdjieff who did not restrain his warm compliments to the two cooks at the end of the evening.

Our return to France was on board the *Ile de France,* a superb new steamship whose crossing the Atlantic left me with most pleasant memories. Sometime later, it was necessary to effect the dispersion of all the old residents of the Prieuré.

GURDJIEFF AND NORMANDY

The emptying of the Prieuré of its residents began in 1931, and was an operation completed only in the course of 1933. Those who left chose their own destinations according to their inclinations and their means. The old watchdog of the Prieuré, Eugene Svechnikov, whose name I have mentioned along with his charming wife Elizabeth, had already cast their lot for Normandy long before us, principally to be closer to their son who was undergoing psychiatric treatment not far from Rouen. My mother had not lost contact with the Svechnikovs and corresponded with them. They coaxed us warmly to join them, which we did when it was our turn to leave the Prieuré.

Thus in 1932, my mother, Papoussia, my cousin Irene and I found ourselves in a little Normandy village with the pleasant name of Sotteville-sous-le-Val, near Saint-Aubin-lès-Elbeuf[5] in the department of Seine Infèrieure, while Gurdjieff was little by little installing himself in Paris. One must believe that the pretensions and requirements of men are functions of the possibilities provided by the period in which they live. It is thus that we had to spend some years in our first house totally bare of comfort—with outdoor toilet facilities, no running water, light by oil lamps, coal burners for heat, etc. Nonetheless, no one complained and in the summer we received our first boarders, who evidently left enchanted by their stay since the greater number of them came back the following year.

As I said above, the facilities were outside, and I found myself obliged to neutralise with sulphur the mounds of human excrement which had built up in this poetic spot.

Some of our boarders had the pleasure of being stung by wasps in that nice spot as they were relieving themselves. These ongoing incidents provided the opportunity there to become inured to the impression of the cries shrieked at the rapacious flyers by these victims of the charms of country life. Later, we had the opportunity to move into the 'chateau' of Sotteville. It was a property much larger and with a number of annexes, but the hygienic conditions of the plumbing were also primitive. Little by little, we succeeded in freshening up the chateau, thanks to a number of boarders who were not long in moving in. They came principally from Paris, and of all ages, but they were all in great shape as far as their appetites were concerned.

☙

I did a lot of bicycling during that time, imitating the racers on the Tour de France. I had occasion as well to make several long excursions, and I never forgot to send postcards to my relatives. The criminal affairs of the epoch seized my imagination particularly. Of the great lawyers of the day I admired Maurice Garçon a great deal, but above all Vincent de Moro Giafferi. Each time he had a case in our area I fixed it so I could be in the crowd which filled the courtroom where he pleaded. I drank in his words, and was made ecstatic by his vocabulary and the effects of his gestures, even when the case was insignificant. In the meantime, I had managed to obtain a secondary school diploma in professional studies and worked for a business degree.

☙

To come back to our boarding house, which was in operation only in the summer, but which gave us means to live the rest of the year, my poor mother was at the furnaces *strictu sensu,* since her stoves were rudimentary ones heated by wood. Papoussia spent most of his time in the kitchen garden which he adored above everything. My cousin Irene had charge of the rooms. As for me, I was considered a sort of master of ceremonies; I was an organiser of swimming parties in the nearby Seine, of games of chess and cards, a disk jockey at my convenience, etc. My functions included also looking for boarders at the Pont-de-l'Arche railway station, and driving people to Rouen, either to dancing halls or to the curb of the Rue des Cordeliers (the old red-light district of the city). I accompanied my mother to the markets of Rouen when she went to buy from the fishmongers. We had also a butcher who made home deliveries.

The atmosphere was very good in our pension, where everyone was privileged to four meals per day. People ate around a hosting table. The language which predominated at our 'château' was incontestably Russian. Little by little, we developed a collection of livestock about us. Geese, ducks and chickens cackled to each other while rabbits rested indifferently in their pens. Our dog Nora, a bit hysterical, affectionate but also a bit crazy, was obviously unable to pass for a good guardian. The only telephone in the village was at Leroy's, the grocer. It was in this bucolic setting that Gurdjieff, on his way to Rouen, liked to enter without warning, leaving his entourage, typically of two or three automobiles, outside. G. I. liked to stay at the Hotel Angleterre on the riverfront, a few steps from the Café Victor, well known in Rouen. I used to open the two doors of our old gate for Gurdjieff to let in his Citroën which he parked in the middle of the courtyard. The instant our dog Nora saw him step out of his car, she greeted him by leaping up and down and yapping with joy. Indulging her, Gurdjieff would stroke her stomach with his foot, while she barked and rolled over and over.

Without a doubt Georgivanich's visits were motivated principally by our presence in the village and the state of Papoussia's health which began to decline seriously. G.I.'s stops were of variable duration. In each of his visits he had *zakuski*[6] and drinks in his car. Eventually he made contact with those boarders who had promising aspects. They would go with him to Rouen for other festivities. On two or three occasions he was not above having me tap my mother for a few hundred-franc notes, which were always returned later with royal thanks. Very often G.I. bought chickens for his own use. At the occasion of one of his bargains he found them a bit skinny. 'Doctorsha,'[7] he said sententiously to my mother, 'when one breeds fowl, one does not skimp on their food'. What they were prone to overlook is that at the conclusion of the transaction, it was me who had to perform the ungrateful task of decapitating the chickens on a block, remove their feathers and empty their innards.

✼

During one trip in Normandy, with a small group to which I was attached, G.I. stopped at a very chic restaurant in Vernon well known for its fried fish. As we were finishing our plate of succulent bleak, the head waiter brought us an elegant salad bowl filled to the top with different salads and aromatic herbs. Gurdjieff broke out into a rage upon seeing salad at the end of the meal, according to French usage. He cried out his outrage in the voice of a Turkish guard:

'Salad? Eat after only donkeys and French!'[8]

The headwaiter, in his stiff obsequious style responded: 'Absolutely, sir'.

One evening as Georgivanich left Sotteville by car, a bit tipsy, I was sitting beside him and three others were seated in the back seat of the car. There was a steep hill to climb and many curves to negotiate before getting onto the national route which led to Rouen. I noticed suddenly with alarm that the car was zigzagging more and more during the climb. 'Let me drive, and rest a while,' I suggested. 'Jerk! Don't you realize that I am warming up the engine'. Another time, when Gurdjieff was spending the night at the Hotel Angleterre after a heavy evening of drinking in a very jovial company, he asked me, as was his custom, to have his car greased and the oil changed. The car was not ready at the promised hour when we arrived at the garage. To kill time waiting for the work to be finished, G.I. and I went to a local cinema where a Fernandel film was being shown. At certain moments Gurdjieff broke out in fits of laughter, without the least concern for the other patrons who were engrossed in the hardships of the actor on the screen.

Papoussia's health was failing further and further, and I realize today how great his stoic suffering was. His prostate cancer had progressed and caused him great suffering. Georgivanich stopped by more often, visibly preoccupied by the state of the health of his most faithful and valuable collaborator. He tried to spoil Papoussia by every means. One day, when Papoussia let him know that he would appreciate some fruit juice, cases full of juice arrived on Gurdjieff's orders. Some time later in 1937, according to his habit, Gurdjieff arrived in Sotteville on his way to Rouen. After the customary small talk, and after greeting Papoussia, there was a brief discrete consultation apart with my mother, whom he had drawn aside. I guessed right away that what they were talking about concerned me directly, and I was not mistaken. To both my surprise and my satisfaction, G.I. had need of me in Paris for a few months, mainly to help him take care of his domestic affairs. I ran to Papoussia to tell him the news, and I saw him break out in tears in front of me. After drawing me into his arms, he gave me a sign to leave him. This scene moved me enormously. To this day I cannot not yet understand the true sense of his great sorrow. That same evening, Monsieur Prunier, the father of my boyhood girlfriend Fernande, took me in his car to Paris by way of Meudon.

PARIS
Rue des Colonels-Renard

'Never follow the flock.'
'Do all that you can also not do.'
Помни себя (*Pomni sebia*).

Virtually untranslatable from Russian, if only by paraphrase. That is to say: 'stay constantly vigilant, conscious of your gestures and your acts, control your compulsions and your interior centres'. 'Eveil à soi-même' (or 'awaken oneself'), which I found somewhere in writings on Gurdjieff[9], seems unsatisfactory. This formula covers the idea of continuity and perseverance in efforts and conscious acts. It is precepts like these which I heard often in G.I.'s close entourage, and which I tried to put into practise myself.

In being with him for the first time in 1937 I lost no time to get acquainted with his place. The apartment seemed spacious at the time. Nevertheless, when I saw it again years later after the death of Georgivanich, I was surprised to imagine how I could have moved about, slept and served G.I. over a period of several months in lodgings which I found now surprisingly small and uncomfortable. When I arrived I found Valentin, alias Valia, Gurdjieff's nephew[10], who showed up a few times each week. Needless to say, the greater part of our work consisted in buying, preparing and serving the midday and evening meals. Food occupied an important part in the life at Rue Colonels-Renard.

My workday began normally at 8:00 in the morning and ended often around 11:00 at night because, in the beginning, I slept in the salon of the apartment, set off by a screen. Georgivanich neither frightened nor put me off in any way. He was perfectly relaxed in my company. He slept most of the time in his underwear. Each time I saw or heard him go toward the bathroom in the early hours of the morning and blow his nose in the oriental fashion, that is to say loudly, pinching his nostrils alternately, I could not restrain a shrug of the shoulders. When later in the morning he went again to the bathroom and gargled, close by, I showed my disapproval with a stiff look. He did not care the least.

In the morning, Gurdjieff was usually satisfied with just a cup of strong black coffee, sometimes with a biscuit and a glass of water. That did not hold him back from lighting his Russian cigarettes even before eating. He was as demanding a schoolmaster when it came to the way his bed was to be made, which surprised me because I deemed this detail absolutely secondary. A fine appearance and clothing fashion were the least of his concerns. He attached no importance whatsoever to what he wore, though he changed his underwear often. His wardrobe was reduced to the bare minimum. The same was true of his shoes, socks ties, hats, handkerchiefs, etc. He disliked shaving and did it only by a sense of obligation. I pressed his trousers from time to time, sewed on buttons, and did even the little daily tasks of mending. I carried out the dirty linen and his shirts to the local laundry, and he gave me full leeway to carry out domestic chores. Little by little, I groomed myself into being his executive right-hand man.

This is the way things would go, for example, in the evening. I would park his automobile, a current model Hotchkiss, on the Rue Brunel. Then I would fetch his mail from the box, read it to him, and sometimes translate important official letters. In the beginning, my sleep was troubled by the murmurs or the giggles of women who took part in the almost nightly parties which G.I. seemed to appreciate so much as any connoisseur of nocturnal pleasures. His sexual potency absolutely astounded me. A propos, about once a week I would cross paths in the apartment with a certain Olga, who had a sly and furtive look, and was obviously the recruiter of pretty young girls. Before going to sleep I always left a thermos bottle full of mocha by his bed. In the salon, as I retired graciously from the scene behind my screen, I would catch a sight of the attractive faces, tableaux vivants in the process of being prepared for the evening. More and more bothered and at the end of my patience, I took Gurdjieff aside one day before his afternoon nap and told him without equivocation that I would prefer to spend my nights anywhere else than Rue Colonels-Renard. At first he gave me a look of irritation but then the lines of his face relaxed almost immediately into a smile full of affability. We had perfectly understood one another! The same day, I moved my meagre belongings to the Hotel d'Armaille, a modest hotel on the street of the same name, a few metres away.

∽

I have already spoken of the importance meals played in the daily routine, and the shopping for goods for their preparation. I wondered often how Georgivanich managed to have so many people every day at his table both for noon and evening meals. He needed this unbroken flow of conviviality, loud voices, toasts, etc. From all appearances, he fled solitude and acted genuinely unhappy when he found himself at the table only in the company of one or a few boring relatives.

Soon after my arrival in the apartment, in my company, Gurdjieff charged his nephew Valia to roast four appetizing capons in the oven. 'Uncle' was expecting some important guests at noon. I enjoyed joking with Valia, and while the master was out somewhere, we relaxed in the salon where we got along like old buddies. What was to be avoided at all costs that day unfortunately came about when we forgot completely about the capons in the oven. I saw Valia leap straight up from his seat and run to the kitchen, only to return with a disconsolate face. At that very moment I heard the key turn in the lock. G.I. came in through the entry with his guests without the least pause. Valia, eyes ablaze, grabbed me by the shoulders and begged me to tell his uncle the bad news. It had to be done quickly. Without changing the expression on my face, I went up to Georgivanich and whispered in his ear: 'There's bad news. We forgot to take the chickens out of the oven!'

Mastering his rage and his disappointment, Gurdjieff strode off toward the kitchen. 'Triple assholes you are. Take the chickens out of the oven immediately,' he roared. With a quick twist of his hand, G.I. tore off the skin which stuck to the burnt carcasses of the birds. A few spoonfuls of butter, some cream, onion, garlic powder and some spices transformed into a delicacy what was a hopeless disaster a few moments ago. I could not believe my eyes. Turning to his nephew, he said: 'Serve this in a crown of basmati rice. This will be a Georgian specialty like *chokhom bili*.'

წ

Gurdjieff and I often did our shopping in the local markets not far from Place **Saint-Ferdinand**. We were a sight at the butchers when G.I., oblivious to others, sliced directly out of sides of beef and lamb the cuts he wanted, without in the least shocking the proprietor of the shop. At that time, whole carcasses hung at the butcher's for the clientele to see. You can imagine the looks on the faces of those who witnessed such behaviour for the first time! Georgivanich liked most of all lamb and veal. Nonetheless, we often bought fowl and fish according to our moods. The boiling and roasting ritual in the kitchen was virtually invariable at Gurdjieff's.

Before leaving his apartment for the Café de la Paix, G.I. would ask for a large sort of basket, which he would fill later with large globs of butter, add some meat specialties of the day, and some spices to go with it. The rest, the vegetables, salads, snacks, were my business. Like most Caucasians, Gurdjieff adored fresh herbs and asked for them year-round. I discovered a good Corsican green grocer on the Boulevard Pereire where every day I would find fresh mint, estragon, parsley, large round onions, garlic, etc. I served him all these things on a large platter at each meal.

One day, despite my searches in the area I could not find the fresh mint he particularly liked. He called me out of the kitchen and began to berate me, fury in his eyes. I confronted him straight-faced without blinking, clenching slightly my teeth (I add parenthetically that for a long time I had built up an emotional armour which took the worst thrusts of G.I.'s rage). He usually stopped yelling, realizing that his cries were futile once the torment he had intended for me had been inflicted. Be it as it may, he was the first to turn away, realizing apparently the futility of continuing the exercise. I guess that my detachment and calm disarmed dear Georgivanich a bit more each time he let loose his anger.

Each day I tried continually to make the most of the good principles which he had instilled in me. I had, so to speak, assimilated the essential core of his teaching. With a poker face, Georgivanich observed and encouraged me in my efforts and in the exercises which I performed on my own. I invented them myself, and I was able to do them well, leaving aside the pleasures of idle reading, stuffy theories and abstract reasoning. My exercises were as much mental as physical, and were directed above all to make my acts conscious and subordinate to my will. The exercises in question would certainly seem quite modest and simple in the eyes of some. I regret that.

It was generally in the morning that I would tell Gurdjieff everything I had accomplished, whether the results were successful, half-successful or, in a word, failures. I never had the impression that G.I. listened to me only for my pleasure. He followed attentively my accounts, nodding his head, smiling, asking questions, etc. I began passing notes to him which summed up my little secrets. For example, and very generally, the exercises can be reduced to a few acts of self-discipline as follows:

'You put on your left sock instead of the right one when you get up'.

'You make three steps forward and one to the side, your toothbrush behind your ear (ten times)'.

'You serve the table with your left hand all day'.

'You keep a stupid smile on your lips without stop for two hours'.

'You speak your first words of the day at a particular time'.

'You take upon yourself to fast completely for two days', etc.

In the beginning, the presence of Valia at his uncle's was mainly to assure meals abundant enough for five or six persons, and which were served on G.I.'s return from the Café de la Paix. After a couple of false starts on Valia's part, Gurdjieff charged me with the fixing of a midday meal to which he had invited a number of people. In the course of doing the shopping rounds, I was chagrined to note that most of our habitual suppliers had changed their policies toward us. One would even say they had banded together. Despite promises and my insistence, all of them who had sold us things on credit, refused categorically to serve me, because, it seems, we were in debt up to our necks. Under these circumstances, I decided to go willy-nilly to the Café de la Paix to bring Gurdjieff up to date on the situation.

'Oh, shit!' he groaned, and then recomposed himself quickly, and said to me:

'Postpone lunch one hour, or more if necessary. We'll serve meatballs. Buy some ground meat and improvise the rest'. He handed me sixty francs, adding that he would shear two or three sheep before tomorrow to put us back in the swing of things. I should mention here that Gurdjieff had set himself a principle that he followed scrupulously. 'You see,' he would tell me from time to time, 'I'll go broke today and tomorrow I'll make some more money'.

It was not unusual to see Gurdjieff borrow money at the Café de la Paix from the waiters, all of whom had known him for a long time. These discrete transactions did not at any time seem dishonourable or even indecent to them. They knew too well Mr Bonbon, his sumptuous gifts as well as the lordly tips which had become legendary. The waiters at the café could only congratulate themselves, since their modest loans would reap huge gains.

I was able to get Valia to give up everything and come to help me. Together we were able to prepare dozens of meatballs in record time, and the hors-d'oeuvres were all ready. Everything went without a hitch that afternoon. Gurdjieff was in particularly good form. There were six guests at the table. With his eyes sparkling with malice, G.I. joked continuously, making suggestive and amusing gestures. There was a young Turkish woman at the table with lovely eyes, and she broke out in bursts of laughter at regular intervals as she listened to Gurdjieff tell her short anecdotes in her native tongue.

I was able to witness a similar episode another time with a beautiful Greek who also seemed to delight in G.I.'s jokes in her own language. Nonetheless, the master had an enormous linguistic handicap which prevented him from expressing himself as he would wish. It is true that he mastered Armenian and Russian perfectly, though he spoke with a decided Caucasian accent. He had undeniable familiarity with Turkish, Greek, Georgian, and, to his great credit, I've been told by others, rudimentary knowledge of various Asian languages. But, alas, his knowledge of English and French was restricted to a scant few words and expressions. His grammar, syntax and vocabulary were unique to him alone.

We would often go to the Turkish baths or a sauna on the Rue des Rosiers, along with Valia and other acquaintances. Georgivanich liked to relax and have a massage in these places where he felt pleasurably at ease. For grand occasions we directed our steps to the well-known restaurant Chez Prunier to eat crayfish. To be sure, G.I. was unmatched as a giver of his famous bonbons which he kept in reserve in his pockets. Mr Bonbon was notorious. Those delicious bonbons, often with fillings, sometimes pure chocolate, were made in Estonia and imported by Fazer, a well-known Finnish sweets maker. In France, in Paris, they could be found at Fauchon's, or Petrossian's and at other deluxe sweetshops.

&

All guests who had the honour of crossing the threshold of the apartment at Rue Colonels-Renard knew perfectly well the celebrated pantry displaying an inimitable assortment of foods and drinks which Georgivanich never stopped supplementing with purchases of new specialties. In fact, this closet-display became a genuine attraction. One could begin with the sight of *baklava, rahat-loukoum,* and *halvah;* and, few were those who knew of the innumerable exotic fruits which Gurdjieff had discovered who knows where. Such rarities could never be found on display on the street. Their price was high, of course. Few people at that time had seen or tasted lychees, guavas, kumquats, papayas, kiwis, and so forth, which arrived from the four corners of the earth, carefully wrapped in wadding or even in jewellery boxes! At certain meals, in the presence of particular guests who were pointed out to me by G.I., by a pre-arranged order or cryptic sign, I would bring in for dessert the most rare produce from Mars or from Mount Ararat. According to the circumstances, after a blow with a wooden mallet in the kitchen to liberate them, I had the privilege of serving on a tray with infinite care and ceremonial flourish, exotic fruits found nowhere else in Paris. Do you wonder whether I am serious or kidding? To believe it or not is not my problem. The point is that the effect looked for was achieved: wide-eyed wonder and squeals of surprise. Stifling my own laughter, I would see it every time.

∞

Four or five times, satisfied with my service, Gurdjieff would exclaim to me as I left him for the night:

'Take the car and go have fun.'

He had entire confidence in me, knowing that I was not prone to alcohol or drugs, and that I smoked only irregularly. Despite the fatigue accumulated throughout the day, I would go sometimes by foot to the amusement park at Porte Maillot and mix with the thick crowd idling there. The spot was noisy, amusing and offered all sorts of attractions. I remember one modest show, but quite exciting for all to see. It consisted of a quite cute young girl, lying in a bed placed on a platform. We could only see her face between the blankets. The man who ran the show passed out cloth balls to whoever wished to throw at her on the platform. Each time one of these balls hit the target, a good distance away, the young girl would leap from her bed in the skimpiest of dress, wiggle her hips a few moments before the aroused spectators, and then disappear again beneath the blankets.

I would also go by car to Pigalle, Montparnasse or Montmartre to relax in my own fashion. I was drawn to the Russian cabarets, less expensive and more authentic in those days. I went occasionally to 'Monocle', a lesbian nightclub where I was not at all ill at ease. It was a place where I drifted almost without thinking of it. The atmosphere was pleasant and calm. Outside before the entrance, there stood a sort of female huckster, dressed in a tuxedo, who rustled up a clientele with a tipsy voice. Seeing me arrive, she would greet me every time with a very friendly smile. Inside, I had fun watching pairs of succubi and incubi tenderly twined together, dancing inoffensively with languid grace.

༄

Naps after meals and drinks at lunchtime were sacrosanct for Gurdjieff. Everyday I would see him go to his bedroom and fall off into a deep sleep almost immediately after his guests had departed. One day, unexpectedly, around 3:00 in the afternoon I heard the doorbell ring again and again, and then an incessant knocking on the door of the apartment. Angry, I raced to the door, opened it carelessly and said to the intruders that Gurdjieff was not available. I was about to close the door when one of the men (there were three) blocked the door with his foot and with excellent French in an arrogant tone, said:

'The master has fixed a rendezvous for us. Let us in at once'.

Without waiting for a reply they stormed into the salon and took places at their ease. I was not the kind to recognize any celebrities of the day, or even know their names. From all appearances, though, these were important people. After a few seconds musing over their possible identities, I was able to attach tentative names to the three guests, but since I was not absolutely certain, I restrained from judgment on the spot. It seemed likely that these were two writers and a famous actor. Without my heart in it, I went to waken Georgivanich. I had to shake him for some time, but as he came to his senses, with his eyes opening, I explained that there were three visitors in the salon who were waiting impatiently to see him. Since he was wearing long underwear, I handed him his slippers and a bathrobe. Seeing him enter, the visitors got up as one, bowed with respect and glued their eyes to him.

'Tell them to join me at the Café de la Paix late in the afternoon', Gurdjieff said to me. I did this and the three left immediately. G. I. seemed still somewhat asleep after his nap, a bit pathetic and vulnerable.

∞

The few rare occasions when I saw him return alone (usually when he went out alone in the evening, he would let me off much earlier), he was in a bad mood. Under such circumstances the bonds between us were much tighter, marked by simplicity and, I am sure, reciprocal affection. He was visibly ill at ease staying in one place. Sometimes he took his little portable harmonium, isolated himself in the salon and spent a good hour improvising melodies which were always a little sad. He had, all the same, retained many oriental habits. This is to say that I saw him pace back and forth, hands clasped behind his back, fingering his beads. I rarely saw him with a book in his hands. I had often to remind him of down-to-earth matters. I had to point out the suppliers whose accounts were to be paid right away.

I brought him up to date on our debts in the area, etc.

Once he asked me to give him an injection in the buttocks. I had a very limited talent in that sort of thing. 'Give me a shot', he said, pointing out with his finger the exact spot for the needle. Despite my desire to do the job, the needle just would not go in correctly. It hurt him and drew blood.

'For God's sake!' he screamed and tore the syringe from my hands. Lying on his stomach he wiped the discoloured spot with ether for a while and plunged the needle in his buttock. It remained for me only to empty into him the contents of the syringe, which I did. His mood softened immediately, and he asked me where I was with my *pomni sebia*. Occasionally relatives came to see him, and were received with his habitual hospitality. Dr Hambachidze, whom I invited from time to time, a charming old man, a surgeon well known in Georgian nationalist circles in Paris, I liked a good deal.

I have not had the occasion to mention Dr Salmanoff who had administered to Lenin, treating him in the old fashioned way with prescriptions of seaweed. There were also little known painters, musicians on the dole, many Caucasians down on their luck, all of whom were familiar with the natural bounty of G.I. The master helped them out financially as best he could.

༄

Since I spent several hours each day in the kitchen, I often received visits there, both by guests whom I knew, one of which was Solita Solano whom I liked despite her lesbianism. There were, by the way, many of the same inclination who gravitated toward G.I., sometimes in a group and sometimes alone. Generally, they were all very nice.

From time to time I was visited by Gabo, a friendly

Caucasian and professional bridge player as well known as the white unicorn, who followed in Gurdjieff's wake many years ago. He would appear in my kitchen after coming up the service staircase. He was a teller of funny stories who visited me as a friend; however, he had the nasty habit of stealing pieces of meat from the platter I was carrying into the dining room.

One day while Valia and I were discussing things in our famous kitchen, G.I. told us he would drive us to Vichy. In short, he was offering us a few days of vacation to release us from the routine. To my surprise, we were only three of us going, G.I. at the wheel, Valia and I. Gurdjieff had a remarkable visual memory particularly concerning places or towns he had passed through several times. We arrived in Vichy without incident and Gurdjieff dropped us off in front of the hotel that he had chosen for us, while he had decided to take a room elsewhere. Vichy is not a big town and for amusement Valia and I went to the spa and mingled with those taking cures. We were sitting on a public bench making idle conversation and laughing without paying any attention to those about us when we saw G.I. walking past, hands in his pockets of his light coat, a soft hat on his head, and in an obvious fit of bad humour. He gave us a strange look but neither stopped nor said a word. He was bored stiff, that was sure. Valia and I wondered what had led Gurdjieff to come all the way here just to impose upon himself such a dull and useless vacation. To this day I cannot understand it.

∞

One evening in Gurdjieff's apartment I met the vice-countess Ksenia de Nozzolini. She was a Slavic beauty, of middle stature, well-formed, frank, gay and full of temperament. Ksenia attracted me immediately. On her side, she treated me right away with unfeigned affection. She came more than once to Gurdjieff's along with her sky terrier, a pet that bothered the master a good deal, because Ksenia had spoiled him. In the kitchen I gave something to drink and eat to this animal who, once out of his mistress' sight, never made things difficult. The **vicomtesse** had lodging at the Claridge the year round. As other guests had done, Ksenia in her turn came to visit me stealthily in the kitchen. 'Come see me at the hotel. I have a proposition for you', she said one day. At this point I should mention that Ksenia, over her real eyelashes, had false ones which gave her a bewitching look. As I learned afterwards, Ksenia was a sub-contractor for Elizabeth Arden and a sort of walking advertisement. When they went on the market at last, her lashes were called Xenocils, but they needed obviously more publicity. Ksenia received me with great kindness at the Claridge and said right away that she had chosen me as a demonstrator, a sort of animated publicity. So I started to idle away my time at Fouquet's on the Champs Elysées, as close as possible to the pedestrian traffic, blinking my eyes for all to see with a detached and studied demeanour. Inevitably, unable to resist, both accompanied and solitary women would stop, fascinated in front of yours truly, and ask me questions. Naturally I kept Ksenia informed of my other minor activities. She spoiled me all the time and how we laughed together often! Another time, she made a rendezvous with me at Claridge's to offer me a cup of hot chocolate. Arriving on her floor I found the door to her apartment ajar. Sensing my presence, she cried out from the bathroom:

'It's you, pet? Come, come rub Ksenia's back.'

ಬಿ

The day finally arrived when Georgivanich told me

quite simply: 'Your mother asks for you. She needs you in the country. You can leave when you wish'.

My turn with Gurdjieff had come to an end. It was Michel de Salzmann who succeeded me.

☙

Papoussia's cancer of the prostrate had advanced without pause. In 1938, the poor man had undergone a painful and crippling operation, as operations were often at that time. His courage was exemplary. He was himself a doctor and who could know better how to judge his own health? The operation had made him bedridden. Drains, probes, catheters, were his daily lot, and the whole business was associated with intolerable pain. A short time before he died, his strength completely sapped, and somewhat due to my mother's insistence, Papoussia asked for a priest. Mother called in Father Leperovsky, whom she knew, from Meudon, near Paris. Leperovsky was a educated man, intuitive, intelligent and very tactful. He had even studied medicine. He confessed Papoussia and gave him last rites. I saw my mother in tears, bent over the inanimate body of her husband, blessing him and crossing herself. Papoussia's face was exceptionally serene and totally relaxed after all the suffering he had endured.

'My poor man, my poor dear martyr', she murmured between tears.

The remains of Papoussia reposed in our dining room. Those close to him watched over him before the burial which took place in the cemetery of Sotteville-sous-le-Val. Many people came the day of the burial, including G. I. of course.

In his funeral prayer, the priest Leperovsky recalled notably, raising his voice and hammering his words home: 'Doctor de Stjernvall died a real Christian. He had rediscovered his faith, peace in his soul and the strait path after many years of servitude and straying'.

I saw Gurdjieff leading the way, out of the mortuary, backing out, his face contracted in discomfort. He could not resist reprimanding my mother for having called in the priest Leperovsky.

༄

Georgivanich cut down severely his trips to Normandy after the death of Papoussia. I saw Gurdjieff again several times in Paris in his apartment and at the Café de la Paix. I noticed that he had new disciples, and the number did not cease to increase as time passed.

༄

Without any doubt, my readers have noticed that in my succinct narrative, coloured by episodes I have lived through, evoked in an inconsistent order the teachings of Gurdjieff, properly speaking, have only been touched upon lightly. I have restrained myself intentionally from delving into abstract and scholarly exegesis. Others more competent than I am will undertake that task, if they have not already done so. In my recollections of Georgivanich, I have kept to the man, the mortal or, more exactly, to the anecdotal side of things. 1877 is the offcial date of birth appearing on Gurdjieff's passport, but before certain of his intimates he pretended that he was born eleven years earlier. Is this but one more of his numerous pranks? Go find out!

Certainly, there are many more things to recount, but I prefer to avoid prolixity. I would have the few pages I present above to my readers have some of the 'survivors' who have not forgotten everything smile.

Be it as it may, I pause here in putting a final point to

my prose. I wish only to add: 'I'll see you soon in the next world, my dear Father Gurdjieff!'

OTHER MEMORIES

I propose now to recall a few episodes in which I was directly implicated. They belong to a large extent to the personality of Gurdjieff, to his role as a guide and a master in the real sense of the term. In this order of ideas I believe it necessary to share with my readers, as faithfully as possible, a few recollections that my mother confided in me both orally and in writing. It seems logical that I should begin with the memorable exodus from Russia, planned and executed by Gurdjieff in which my mother, Elizaveta de Stjernvall, participated. I allow her to recall the experience in her manner, with simplicity.

ACROSS THE CAUCASUS WITH G.I. GURDJIEFF
by Elizaveta de Stjernvall

I

The end of the year 1916 was full of signs of grave imminent events. Nonetheless, the extent of the changes in political structures in which we were inevitably involved, were not noticed by us at all.

I was living then in Saint Petersburg where my husband practised psychiatry. Even as an adolescent my husband felt attracted to what some classified under the term 'eternal questions'. He sought to discover the sense of our period of life on the earth; he wished to know the Truth, to recover God and to continue to question what we are and what awaits us after life.

All these obsessive questions pushed my husband inevitably to associate with others plagued by the same questions. Among these was P.D. Ouspensky, whom my husband had met in the intellectual milieu which attracted him at this time. In fact, Ouspensky made it known to my husband very soon that he knew an exceptional person, to whom a certain Caucasian sculptor, Mercurov, had introduced him in Moscow. This personality, Ouspensky added, was undoubtedly the only one who could provide an answer to the different questions which preoccupied my husband. It was thus that we learned that G.I. Gurdjieff, boyhood friend of Mercurov, was in Moscow and would soon make an appearance in Saint Petersburg.

The arrival in Saint Petersburg of Gurdjieff was of great interest for us, and we awaited impatiently for an occasion to meet him. This came about in due course when my husband and I were invited to a meeting which brought us into the company of the master.

When we arrived where his lecture was being given, we found the room already full, and we noticed, looking about us, a man of middle age, medium build, tanned either by race or the sun, with a particularly penetrating gaze.

Gurdjieff greeted each of us very warmly and courteously. Then he joined us in listening to one of his disciples read the first lesson intended for us. This course outlined in a way the essential principles of the teaching of Gurdjieff. I will not speak of it except in summary fashion in this account, which exposes rather our later exodus from Russia and our memorable expedition across the mountains of the Caucasus. At any rate, I will try to give a synthesis of this first lecture I attended.

It concerned most of all the automatism habitual in man which keeps him from being conscious of his acts. Modern man reveals himself only by acts informed by exterior influences. His judgments are always partial, and so, wrong. In order to aspire to a harmonious development of his being, man must, above all else, put his three centres to work simultaneously at the instant each of the functions of his psyche come into play. The force of these three centres—mental, emotional and motor—must be of equal intensity. It is only in this case that the three operating parts of the human machine which we are will work with regularity without impeding one another. To this end, man must struggle with all his strength against his faults and his weaknesses and develop in himself new faculties.

These few theories of Gurdjieff's which I have just exposed very briefly will give the reader an idea of the teaching to which my husband and I adhered. Of course, it is not my intention to dwell excessively on the teaching in question, for my purpose is only to describe our Master in his most human aspect. Thanks to his extraordinary clairvoyance, his intelligence, and his grasp of events, he changed completely the course of my life as well as the life of my husband. Gurdjieff allowed us, simply, to escape from the 'paradise' of the Bolsheviks.

Gurdjieff's stay in Saint Petersburg was not long, but in a few days he was able to talk separately with all those who showed interest in his ideas, and to come to an opinion about each of us. Before leaving us, he asked if we were disposed to follow his teaching. He gave the responsibility to Ouspensky to organize periodic meetings for us. As for himself, he returned to Moscow where he had taken up residence.

II

The beginning of 1917 did not afford us much leisure. It was clear that something extraordinary was about to take place in Russia, particularly in Petersburg. As for me, very young at the time, I could not imagine the extent of the events which would engulf us and make us think of fleeing Russia. The presence of my parents and all my friends in Petersburg dissuaded me from any idea of flight. Things took their course until September 1917. One day, however, my husband received a telegram from Gurdjieff whose message was the following: 'Leave aside all your current affairs and liquidate your assets. Take your way to the south of Russia this month'. This unexpected and laconic message put us in a state of panic, but my husband kept repeating to me that we should follow to the letter the instructions of Gurdjieff who knew and understood what none of us were in position to understand. Of course, it was impossible for us to liquidate everything in our possession in so short a time, but we did our utmost, and at the beginning of October we were able to leave Petersburg under relatively normal conditions. As to our large baggage, which was, unfortunately, sent off late, the Bolsheviks seized it as they seized power two weeks later.

Our objective was to reach Sochi, where Gurdjieff had already moved with his family and a dozen disciples.

Our Master had rented in the Sochi area a beautiful property on the Black Sea. Alas, we did not have the opportunity to spend much time in this charming place. Each morning, in effect, Gurdjieff went down to the shore, spending many minutes looking at the sea to assure himself, according to the movement of the ships, of the development of the political situation. Realizing that the Bolsheviks had already succeeded in moving closer to our situation, the order was given to pack bags and look for another refuge on the coast, more distant from populated areas. A few days later, we were able to find a house that acquaintances put at our disposition. Nevertheless, in looking over the furniture and the atmosphere dominating our new residence, we understood easily that there, also, our stay would be provisional. Our fears were rapidly confirmed by another decision of Gurdjieff, who now decided that we should go to the north of the Caucasus.

The place of our Master's choice was Essentuki, a well-known spa where we were sent post haste with the mission to find a suitable place to live. We arrived at Essentuki without much trouble and had the good fortune to find a house in good order, large and comfortable, in which we settled right away. Each family had access to a room, since the upper floor had large conference rooms. As soon as we arrived, we posted a sign on the wall of the house with the following inscription: 'International Alliance of Ideological Workers'. This label, it must be said, fit perfectly the spirit of the times, for the Bolsheviks did not take long to pay us a visit in which they asked questions about our aims and the activities of our association.

Our life in Essentuki went along in a more orderly fashion than before, and each of us had an assigned job to do. Our financial resources, on the other hand, dwindled day by day, for we were already close to a score in number, and Gurdjieff had to expend all his energy to assure our livelihood. Soon after our arrival in Essentuki, our Master felt obligated to sort out the men which composed our group and ordered the engineers, lawyers and accountants chosen to go look for work in the enterprises of the town. These enterprises for the most part, were already running under Bolshevik control. Our companions had no trouble entering into occupations and, ensuring our livelihood, made valuable contacts for us among the population and the new powers in control. It did not take long for us to realize not only that the Bolsheviks did not have any animosity as far as we were concerned, but efforts according to their means to accede to our desires. I cite here an episode as example, insignificant in appearance, but which the reader will note to what extent our Master knew how, as one says, to 'seize the moment' to exploit profitably all circumstances.

It needs to be made clear, in effect, that at the epoch in which we found ourselves in Essentuki, a good deal of merchandise became more and more scarce in the shops. Therefore, it was even difficult to find sewing thread or rolls of silk. One day, I saw Gurdjieff carrying toward us a huge basket filled with silk all tangled up which he had bought out in the country. In a few hours, and according to the instructions of our Master, we had organized a veritable workshop where we women had for our task to straighten out and roll up the tangle of silk on pieces of cardboard handsomely fashioned. Gurdjieff came around from time to time to inspect our work and give instructions. At the end of about two weeks our work was completed. I swear that we produced a spectacular result, because merchants literally fought for our precious product.

Twice a week we had meetings in the evening. A large number of people attended, including teachers and scholars who had also chosen exile. In general it was a disciple specially trained and qualified who read the lecture text, but it was Gurdjieff who responded to the numerous questions posed by the most cultured and advanced persons in the audience.

In Essentuki our Master gave us a great deal of time, interviewed each of us, and pointed out to us our shortcomings unable to be recognized ourselves. Often, he assigned us specific tasks whose duration varied. We had among us a woman with her son in his twenties who was very interested in Gurdjieff's teachings. One day our Master called the young man to him and, after having assigned to him just enough money for his travel, he ordered him to leave his mother and to go to another city, from where he was not to return before the end of a week. The young pupil had no practical sense at all, and had, apparently, never faced the realities of life. The assignment consisted of showing him what he was capable of and how he could manage in a new and unknown environment. I must admit that the pupil handled himself very well.

Another of our group had a weakness for good things; she lost all control of herself in front of foods and delicacies for which she had a particular delectation. Without being what one would call a 'big eater', she would automatically swallow without measure whatever pleased her. The self-observation which Gurdjieff imposed for her was not at all easy. It was on visits, she said herself, that she had the most trouble controlling herself, because each time dishes which she preferred were served, she had, using different pretexts, to stop herself suddenly from eating, to the great surprise and disfavour of her hosts.

All of these practical exercises, as 'individual tests' of a new sort, produced good results. They forced us to tame our weaknesses, to control the least of our acts and to constantly bring into play our desires.

Throughout each day, many hours were devoted to gymnastics, cooking, housekeeping and music.

III

In Essentuki, our Master constantly reminded us that a long journey to cross the Caucasus lay before us, a journey which would allow us to reach the south and countries beyond. We prepared ourselves, therefore, for our departure with a collective enthusiasm, for life in Essentuki was becoming more and more precarious because of the political situation.

Gurdjieff had ordered all the men of our group, in poor shape physically, to carry each evening a sack of some forty-five pounds on their shoulders and to race at high speed through the house for an hour. Also, without putting down the weight, they had to climb the stairs to the attic and then down to the cellar. All these exercises were to acquire the breath and the physical resistance they lacked. During this time, our companions who worked in different establishments in the city, prepared the field to force the Bolsheviks to hand over to us wagons, shovels, and pickaxes as well as diverse tools that could serve us on the course of our scientific expedition which we put underway under the cover of our proposal to study Caucasian stone monuments.

I must say as well that the women neither remained inactive. They trained as did the men, but with less weighty packs which contained indispensable items such as linen, shoes, etc.

On 7th August 1917 we finally took our route. Our group consisted of seventeen persons. We had to wait a long time for our departure date and put it off frequently because of local political events. Nonetheless, I could never forget that memorable day when, after a thousand difficulties, complications and setbacks, our contingent set off for the unknown in cattle cars.

Three men and two women occupied the first train wagon in which were also the horses, dogs, bench carts and various other objects. The rest of our group occupied the other car where a Russian cart was placed along with the heavy baggage. Our intention was to reach Tuapse on the Black Sea where we would unload our wagons, then continue our route on foot across the mountains. Our equipment consisted mostly of sacks, containing the most indispensable objects, which we loaded on our horses or carried on our backs, according to the situation at hand.

The night in Armavir passed without incident, and the next day our wagons were moved toward a little station which was still accessible. The same day, Gurdjieff assigned us different tasks. One of us was charged with finding and preparing food. Another was to tend to the animals, a third to the horses. This last assignment, to see after the horses' well-being, was mine. My job obliged me to spread straw in our make-shift stable.

Having arrived at the end of our voyage by rail, we spent three days on a siding waiting for an opportunity to get on our way again. Days passed quickly, each of us had our appointed tasks to do. We made our meals outside near the wagon. After a three days wait we heard that the route we wanted to take was still blocked. We had to consider staying where we were for better or for worse, and my husband went to look for a place to live. It was futile to expect to find something in the city which was over-stacked with people. With nothing better at hand we moved into a reserve military barracks. The countryside spread out before us was lovely to behold—fruit trees in abundance and, at our feet, the Belaya River. As for comfort, of course, we had none at all. We spent the first night in the little guard house sleeping on boards which had previously served as shelving. The next day we were able to move into a small house of three squalid rooms without any furniture. Gurdjieff moved into one, the women had another and the men had the third. We all slept on the floor, just as we had done in the wagons. At 6:00 in the morning everyone was up and each attended to his job. We led our horses, as they grazed along the way, to the river. The women tended them in three-hour shifts. We ate outside, seated on a rug in front of the house, taking our food from common bowls placed in our midst. During the day we were free to spend time on our private affairs without, nonetheless, forgetting the individual problems of which I spoke earlier. Considerations of the outside world were rare.

One day I saw three monks come by, or, more exactly, three hermits. They were members of a sect eager for spiritual nourishment. They had heard tell of our Master and wanted to make his acquaintance. They met on the grass where we all sat. We followed with interest the remarks exchanged before us, but, for all intents and purposes, the new audience had trouble following. To my regret, I was present only at the end of the meeting and cannot record all of it. I remember questions about vegetarian diets and the immortality of the soul. Gurdjieff's answers, as usually happened before uninitiated listeners, completely baffled the monks. He said simply that immortality for beings without a soul, with only a physical coating, was but a myth. To aspire to immortality, one must be impregnated with a more subtle substance contributing to an astral and mental body.

We spent several days waiting for the chance to continue our journey. The political situation was unfavourable for us. We found ourselves in a dead end, not far from

Maykop, but we were reduced to complete immobility. Often at night we heard shots fired and the deafening echo of artillery and other unsettling noises. Patrols armed to the teeth sometimes ventured right up to us, and soldiers, with their arms laden with pillaged goods, passed by the camp. To tell the truth, the scene before our eyes was hardly peaceful and more than once we regretted having left Essentuki. It was only our shakeable faith and blind confidence in Gurdjieff in everything he undertook that allowed us to surmount the anguish and discouragement that filled us.

Monotonous days passed, for we saw practically no one. From time to time, we were visited by a rather strange person with a thick red mop of hair who called himself a Buddhist monk, and who appeared half naked with bare feet. Obviously he enjoyed our company, but to get to us he had to ford the river that separated our residences. In order to do so, he undressed on the opposite shore, put everything in a huge hat he wore and then nimbly stepped into the water. When he saw the women he cried out 'Don't look, don't look!' We knew little about this man. Someone said he was Finnish, but the story of his religious order was not clear. Frankly, he was entertaining to us, and he was very interested in Gurdjieff's teaching.

We went to bed at sunset because we had no lighting. Sometimes, when our Master did not get up and leave us early because of an interesting conversation going on, we stayed on around the fire. It was a novel picture and very enticing. To tell the truth, this bohemian life we led brought us all close to one another. Far off there was the turmoil of the war, but all that left us impassive. We lived in our own world, with our own interests and hopes which would appear incomprehensible in the mind of the non-initiated! I hold dear the memory of numerous pleasures from each day we spent like that. I felt I was alive in all senses of the word. I came out of the demoralizing torpor in which I had indulged myself. Furthermore, our life had sense now. We had ceased to grope in the shadows.

IV

On the first of September, after procuring all the necessary papers and safe conducts, our expedition took off again. In the interval, the region where we had taken shelter was the theatre of much combat and had often changed hands. One day we saw an airplane dropping leaflets around us. The text asked for the city population to surrender without resistance under threat of reprisals. Two days later, the city fell into the hands of the Cossacks, to the great disarray of the Bolsheviks who had to retreat in great haste.

The new authorities delivered the authorizations we waited for, and so were finally able to leave behind our camp and take route toward the mountains.

Our departure took place at noon under a torrid sun. Toward evening, harassed by fatigue and gripped by hunger, we entered a town where we spent the night. We were able to find refuge with a Cossack who put terrain around his house at our disposition, as well as pasture for our livestock. After removing the harnesses of the horses, we hurried to prepare our dinner, which was very ample this time, thanks to the milk and bread our host gave us. We slept on straw spread on the grass. Toward 2:00 in the morning, nonetheless, I was already up and, with the person standing guard, went to find water for our samovar. With the first glimmer of dawn, Gurdjieff gave us orders to prepare for departure. Everyone was on his feet in a wink, and very rapidly we got on our way. The path opening up before us was very beautiful. After a few kilometres of march we found ourselves again on a trail covered with green and flanked by majestic peaks. We went along at a good pace, about six kilometres per hour. Near 2:00 in the afternoon we stopped to refresh ourselves.

The long trek on which I was forced to participate, as well as the two previous nights I spent without really closing my eyes, wore me out completely. It was with indescribable difficulty that I was able to drag myself away from the others and drop on a coat I had thrown to the ground. I fell into a deep sleep right away. I sensed that I was at the end of my strength and unable to go another step. To my great surprise, thanks to the meal I put down and the half-hour nap which restored me, I was able to resume the march feeling fresh and rested. Three hours later, after an ascent made difficult by the loads on our backs, we could see Kamenolomsk. Our last climb had been so steep that we had to unload the two carts and carry all the equipment on our backs. As for the women, each carried her own belongings.

A little after arriving in Kamenolomsk, my husband went off to scout around for lodgings. He was lucky to get us into a school comprising two rooms full of desks. Despite all the discomfort we endured, we spent an excellent night on the floorboards, so completely tired out we were. Besides, such conditions no longer surprised us, and we thought it perfectly normal to stretch out on the floor. In truth, it was just a question by now of habit!

Up at 6:00, I went right away to look for bread in the town. The fact was that bread was no longer available in shops, but was made in huts by the inhabitants. The vicissitudes of political order had put an end to all delivery of flour. In all the huts I went into, I met with the same negative response. As for the villagers, they were busy gathering and drying plums and pears. Finally, I entered a little hut a passer-by had pointed out to me. There as well, there was no bread.

The woman into whose hut I had entered was probably in her sixties. She had an open face which radiated health, but I saw right away that she was completely unable to move, having suffered a stroke a month before our coming. She had lost the use of her limbs and could only lie motionless on the bench of her dwelling. Since she was all alone and I had expressed spontaneously my sympathy after she explained her misfortune, she insisted on offering me some fresh butter, all that she had left. I went away with the butter and then, following her directions, went to call on well-off peasants where I was able finally to get bread.

The morning after, our convoy set off toward a new destination. This time I took my place in a bench cart and drove a superb mare, while another disciple took charge of another carriage drawn by two mules. The way was beautiful. Panoramas of indescribable variety followed one after another and we all fell into rapture. The Belaya River snaked without end before us, seeming to catch up to us everywhere. Two hours later we made a stop at Dokhovskaya where my husband, as before, was charged with finding safe-conduct passes. Unfortunately, the assistant of the Ataman had disappeared and he alone was authorized to grant the needed papers. I should remark in passing that our scientific expedition at the time of which I speak, so full of troubles, seemed absolutely mad in the eyes of the masses, and even provoked distrust. For unknown reasons, some attributed to us a political aim, and people whispered as we passed. Finally, after an hour's wait, we went on. Soon after we halted and let our livestock breathe while we took a brief rest. As soon as we began recovering ourselves, we saw four Cossacks galloping toward us. My husband, who got up at the arrival of the riders, and who entered into a discussion with them, came back to tell us that the four Cossacks, for their own security, insisted on a thorough search. First of all were the passports, then our personal effects which were scrutinized, leafed through and closely examined. Once this formality was over, the Cossacks excused themselves brusquely. The fact was that they had been fooled earlier and had let pass some apparently inoffensive persons that they had been looking for intently (that is, Bolsheviks). We learned as well that someone had sounded the alarm in their little town that Lenin and Trotsky were hiding with us!! To have a clean conscience, they had chased after us. The time taken to get through this incident, added to the long search to which we had to submit, prevented us from going further that day. That evening, before going to bed, we feasted on two chickens we had bought on the way. The night was lovely, the place enchanting with moonlight that kept us from sleeping despite our fatigue from the day's events. At some distance from our encampment I saw suddenly the glimmer of a fire and heard the sonorous echo of a song. I wanted very much to go and see what was going on over there, and asked a companion to go with me. A few minutes later we came upon several adolescents who were in a heated discussion with two men from our group. When we were noticed, they made a sign for us to join them. All of them were roasting maize which we tasted with delight. As to our new young friends, they had come there to look for wild pears to trade for bread, and they came in an oxen-drawn cart. The next day, they had to take the same route as ours to ford the river. Frankly we learned something on this new stage in our journey, because of the heavy burden on our animals who were not used to this sort of toil. Since our new companions proposed to come to our aid, we accepted with joy. Higher up we joined the others and spent the night under the stars on a large rug we spread out on the grass.

On awakening we prepared right away to go on. Gurdjieff had allowed the women to cross the river astride the oxen which awaited us by the edge of the water. The river was not very wide, but the bottom was rocky and the current strong. Our crossing was accomplished without the least trouble, thanks to the experience and cool-headedness of our mounts. Once on the other bank, we soon built a fire while awaiting the passage of the others of our group. After about an hour we saw a cart drawn by two mules enter the water carefully. Our Master was on it. Then, after going ahead a few moments, the mules stopped and refused to advance. Gurdjieff began to urge them forward, but in vain. The two beasts obstinately held their place despite being moved by the current. This was a critical moment, for our Master risked being thrown into the water with all the goods aboard. Then some of our men, after taking off some of their clothes, leapt to his aid. Gurdjieff himself had undressed in a wink and jumped down from his seat. With all their combined strength, our men succeeded in getting everything and everybody across safely to the other bank of the river. Our horses, however, gave us no trouble and behaved themselves admirably.

The path that lay open before our wondering eyes was one of the most beautiful I have ever seen. The spectacle was grandiose, with the mountains on one side and the torrential river on the other. Unfortunately, the terrain over which we moved was incredibly rocky and constantly rising. At each moment the members of the expedition had to push the cart with all their strength to allow the horses to advance. Towards evening, completely exhausted, we reached a sort of mountain lookout. We had covered in all only a dozen kilometres since the moment we left our last base. Our new stop discouraged us right away, for besides a half-crazed guard who lived in a shaky little outbuilding, we found nothing useful in this sinister spot. The structure of the building was maintained by planks through which came the plaintive meowing of cats abandoned or imprisoned there by their owners. In despair, we moved into a shed we found in the surrounding area. Then, just as I returned from the river where I refreshed myself, I heard the bad news: the grange was infested with fleas. One woman amused herself by making a count, and found seventy-seven in a few seconds. So, naturally, another night of insomnia, since we were literally eaten alive by these abominable vermin. To forget our misery we set about cooking potatoes and maize over a fire.

Since the day before already we had to be content exclusively with potatoes, not having been able to procure bread. In the morning we set out again on our trek and soon reached a spot on our route where we were forced to abandon our cart. The track was no longer passable. Again we needed a place to stay, and again the only one we could find was a school, this one consisting of two rooms, one of which was used on occasion as a chapel. We moved in all together into one of the rooms while our Master and his wife occupied the teacher's room. The first thing to do was to find bread and other foods. This was an assignment difficult to fulfil, because the peasants themselves lacked almost everything. Political events, among other things, had prevented them from going into town for provisions.

We spent all day sorting out our things to get rid of the fleas and to look for food. The next day a few men and women left with backpacks for the mountain. I stayed in place. In the village the entire populace were busy drying and treating sunflower seeds that they used to produce an excellent oil. We left the village on the third day after having loaded all our equipment on four horses and a sack a piece on our shoulders. As a rule, the men had the job of leading the horses by the bridle while we followed with our burdens. This time I also had to lead a horse with his saddle pack. We advanced with indescribable difficulty. Our backs ached horribly and our sacks shifted constantly. On top of that we had to hold the load of the horses, since they were unaccustomed to carrying a saddle pack on a narrow path.

Soon we had to pause, literally out of breath. The loads we carried on our shoulders were more than our strength could sustain.

Our Master, who observed us one by one and studied our behaviour, freed me from my horse. This was an enormous relief for me, but as the kilometres passed by our strength diminished more and more, and it was with superhuman effort that we succeeded in making the last few meters remaining before the site of our next stop.

We slept this time on some tarpaulin, unable to erect our tents. Still, the route that lay before us the following day was the worst of all. For kilometres we could go forward only through an immense marsh where our poor animals were constantly mired. To our great joy, after leaving this horrible passage, we saw soon a sort of hut before us where we decided to spend the night. Unfortunately, the aforesaid hut was too small to hold all the members of our expedition, but we resigned ourselves to it. We made a fire in our shelter and at sunrise our Master prepared on the hot embers crêpes which we ate with great appetites. A bit later Gurdjieff, accompanied by four men, went back to our old base to bring the rest of our troupe as well as the loads that our animals could not carry on a single trip. During his time away we cleaned our hut with branch brooms and looked about for dry wood. Toward mid-afternoon our men were already back.

We found ourselves at this time at a considerable altitude, as a result of which we suffered from the cold. Our refuge overlooked an entire mountain chain and the panoramic view we enjoyed was of incredible beauty.

The evening passed very pleasantly. In place of bread, still not to be found, our Master made us Greek cakes from flour. He made a hundred which were equally distributed among us.

The next day we were confronted once more with

rough terrain. We often had to jump from rock to rock and unload our horses so they could follow us. A good deal of precious time was thus wasted. I should note here that we had so much baggage that we had no choice but to put into action a system of relays. One part of our group would go ahead while the other would join the first group a day later and rest in wait for the return of the horses. Once more we endured an extremely hard day, and only the majestic and wild beauty of the countryside over which we traversed softened the harsh effort we had to exert. After an interminable descent, during which we had several falls, we finally reached a plateau where we could walk for a while with less strain on our muscles. Suddenly, we found ourselves entangled in brush and lost our path. In effect, we were completely off track. We decided then to split up in order to find the right way. One part of our group left the one in which I was and went off in another direction with our Master at its head. As for us, we found it harder and harder to follow those ahead of us, so encumbered were we beneath the loads on our shoulders. We walked eight hours straight without any rest to speak of. Toward evening we finally managed to regroup, and we saw in the distance the goal we hoped to reach, consisting of huts Armenians lived in. But to get there we had to undertake another descent straight down or find a winding trail. Our horses were so overworked that we could not think of using them further, so we chose the first option. At nightfall we reached the huts, but found them all deserted. Their owners, who were herders and cheese-makers, had left about a week before our arrival. We realized right away that these were precarious lodgings, hastily built and exposed to all winds. Since the nights were cool, however, we were glad to profit from their shelter. To tell the truth, that which mattered the most was to lie down and sleep. As for me, I was beyond feeling fatigue, since I was living on nerves alone. The next morning I awoke in a bad mood, bitter and demoralized, and spent the whole day on my bed. G. I. Gurdjieff, nevertheless, saw nothing serious in my condition, and said it was due to fatigue.

We had once more set up camp in a place which captured us with its beauty. In the evening, when we heated our hut, we retrieved a warm and amicable atmosphere. Each of the small lodges that we occupied had been, without doubt, lived in by an entire family, in judging the objects we found in them. After all the trials we had been subjected to, we could not hope to find better accommodations.

We spent two days in our refuge. On the third, we faced the mountain once more. The first signs of undernourishment were already being sensed by the men as well as by the animals. Hunger gnawed at all of us, and our poor horses lacked forage was well. We ate either potato soup and mushrooms we found in the forest, or gruel. All that we were able to find in that country did not amount to a hill of beans. Besides the multiple hardships of our trek, we had a serious accident. One of our horses was losing his pack on the way and my companion, trying to come to his aid, fell unluckily on an axe and cut himself deeply on the arm. This made us lose a lot of time and our Master's group had already gone on far ahead of us. It was only after covering nearly eight kilometres that we were able to rejoin it. We paused then for a moment to rest and feed the animals. It was then that I noticed some huts at the foot of the mountain where we were. I had the idea of scouting about in hopes of finding some food. So I made a sign to a member of our expedition to follow me, and we went down the slope to the bottom where we reached our goal. In entering one hut we were lucky to find the owner, a man about thirty, he greeted us cordially. He served us sour milk prepared in a particular way, cheese and cornbread. Our host lived in quite unique conditions. His seat was made of boards covered with skins of animals he had hunted. With the exception of one very long bench and a sort of bunk carved of wood, I saw no familiar objects inside. In one corner, however, my eyes fell on large quarters of cheese and barrels of sour milk. Our host, of modest appearance, owned some 500 head of cattle. I was able to buy from him ten kilos of cheese. He had no butter, but on my request, ordered a little boy to make some on the spot.

As I talked with the cattle-raiser, I could not help but notice the skinned body of an animal hanging from a hook. It was a wild goat, and since we had not eaten meat for a week, I asked if I could buy it from him. To my great satisfaction he offered to give me a piece, and then handed over to me the animal's head.

I swear that we left our host entirely sated and proud of our booty. The return was effected under the most deplorable conditions. During the ascent I kept stumbling and stepping on stones which broke under my foot. I had several falls, each time dropping from my hands the some twelve kilos of meat I carried on my shoulder. To complete my mishaps, the heat was unbearable and we sweated profusely. Finally, after unspeakable effort, we found the trail on which we came upon the stragglers who were trying to reunite with the lead group which included Gurdjieff. All of a sudden we were caught up by two Imeretians[11] whom we already knew. They were happy fellows, talkative and helpful, and they escorted us a while. Nevertheless, each time they offered me aid I refused, because I wanted to finish this adventure to the very end myself. As for the countryside about us, it was a constant enchantment which moved us to exclamations of wonder. Toward the end of the afternoon we reached the foot of the Belaya Mountain where Gurdjieff and our other companions awaited us. I saw then that our horses had been unloaded of their packs already, and I guessed that we would camp there. I was right, for I noticed that we were, in fact, in a sort of hamlet where a family of Imeretians lived. They had a herd of cows and raised goats. Since the hamlet was rich in dairy products of all sorts, that evening we had a real dinner: roast baby goat and all the milk we could drink.

We spent the whole next day resting in anticipation of a particularly difficult ascent of Mount Belorechenski to come.

When we left again, our lead group was composed of six people including our Master. From the start, our trajectory promised to be very arduous. We were on a trail flanked by rocks. The vegetation about us was slight and withered, the heat was crushing, and there was no trace of water. We had not eaten since morning and it was almost 6:00 in the evening! We thought to reach the village Babuk, the only place we might expect to find food. Unfortunately, we did not get there despite our haste and the twenty-five kilometres we had covered. Our horses went along with indescribable difficulty, and they lay down as soon as they could by shaking aside their packs. Finally, we spotted a clearing and decided to spent the night there. The group following did not show up. We had left four persons at the hamlet to guard the things we could not carry with us.

We were at the end of our strength. Our Master never ceased from exhorting us to be brave and patient. In order to protect ourselves from wild animals, we built two large fires on the clearing which we tended all night long by turns. The next day my husband went to the nearest hamlet to see if we could stay there and find food. He came back three hours later with good news, having gotten all the necessary promises from the village chief.

The descent towards the hamlet was most perilous because of the number of stones that lay along the slope we had to slide down. The village head put at our disposal magnificent grounds which had every desired quality: sweet grass for our animals and many fruit trees. Then, according to established rule, the first ones arriving at a place had to retrace their steps with the horses relieved of their loads and lead back all those rested behind. Our Master was, in effect, one of those. Nevertheless, of all the men who had arrived with me at our destination, none wished to retrace the same route in the opposite direction. Despite his long hardship, my companion with the cut arm grabbed a horse by the bridle while my husband got up to sacrifice himself in turn. Because I knew he was ailing I suggested taking his place.

The trail that my companion and I had to take this time was, of course, the same, but going uphill. At times our horses went so fast that we had to run, literally, by their sides. We did not know what to do, and I believe I have never had such a hard time in my life. Often I was on the point of bursting into tears, and I begged my companion to stop this wild chase, but the horses, sensing that they were nearing their old pasture, hurried forward even faster. I felt my heart bursting in my chest. This terrible trial must not go on. To add to our discomfort, night was already falling, and we could not see ten paces in front of us.

All sorts of animal denizens of that mountain fled before our onslaught, knocking down tens of stones which we barely dodged. I knew that at any price we had to reach those who were waiting for us, and I had to make a decision on the spot: to stop half-way, or, at the risk of countering the orders of Gurdjieff, get astride a horse which had carried a pack all day long. Without hesitation I stopped my horse and climbed onto his back. I think this manoeuvre saved me because a little later we saw the fires and realized that our friends were not far away. As I arrived I jumped to the ground, hardly able to stand on two feet, and let myself drop onto material on the ground around the camp. My companion, I swear, was no better off than me. Gurdjieff, who waited while the men gathered the horses, showed his displeasure at seeing me like this, but I quickly explained how things had gone. Our master obliged us then to load the horses.

Once preparations were made, Gurdjieff gave the signal to start off. This time I carried a suitcase and held onto a dog by leash, half dead from fatigue. After hardly covering a few meters, our horses, which we had let go ahead as they wished, suddenly left the trail we were following. We began to grope in the dark, then lit lanterns, but all in vain. Evidently the horses were trying to go back. The women asked Gurdjieff to do the same because one of them could see nothing in front of her, and the others were afraid of the dark. Our Master submitted to persuasion and we returned to the place we had just left. Tired as I was, I rejoiced.

The next day we were ready in less than an half hour. At a little distance from the village toward which we were heading, we saw my husband who had come to meet us. But, he did not need to help because the horses were now used to the mountains and went quite well. At our destination we found large grounds in the village put at our disposition by the chief of this little place. Above all, we were happy to be able to heat ourselves and wash in the river which ran not far from where we pitched our tents. During more than three weeks we had slept in our clothes, in effect, and we had to get rid of the fleas.

Most of the villagers were busy drying pears and making *arak*. This drink was made in a simple manner. Softened pears were thrown into a cauldron, and yeast added. Once the yeast began to ferment, distillation was produced by heat. The ethyl vapours rose into an alembic, then condensed under effect of cooling. Someone had me taste this kind of vodka, and I did not particularly like it.

The members of our expedition spent the day picking pears and apples with which they cooked in an oven to make fruit stew.

The day of our arrival in the village, toward evening, we saw the group which we had left at our last base. Our friends were still under the effects of a shocking incident when they had been attacked by brigands who stole all their goods and threatened their lives. The attack had been so sudden that our companions thought at first that they were dealing with harmless hunters. Unluckily the pseudo-hunters, after firing a few shots into the air, fell on the voyagers, surrounded them and had them raise their hands. They were particularly interested in the rifles and pistols our friends carried. Undoubtedly, the bandits were in conspiracy with the herders we had passed on our way and from whom we had bought cheese and milk. After a careful search of our friends, leaving them bereft of everything they thought of value, the bandits left their victims. One woman in the group was very courageous and resolute, and tried to intimidate the brigands, and called for them to return what they had robbed, I must admit that she recovered a part of the loot, but of course our firearms were not returned.

This unforeseen incident lasted at least two hours. Happily, our animals were spared as well as the peasants who accompanied our friends. We mulled this adventure over and resolved in the future to take necessary steps to avoid such aggression to ourselves. The fact was that we always travelled in groups, the first arrived awaited the latecomers and the last leavers.

We spent four days in the charming village of Babuk to recover our strength and satisfy our hunger. Luckily, we were able to buy all sorts of food in that place, including young pigs, lots of milk, and cornbread. But most of us suffered from one thing or another. Some were seriously weakened, others had cuts and blisters on hands and feet. Each day I made bandages for three of our unlucky companions. My husband had a liver ailment and his body was covered with sores.

Our Master made the decision to reduce the length of our walks in order to permit us to be all together once evening came. We retook our march then in conformity with these new instructions.

V

Leaving Babuk, we noticed that our best horse had disappeared. After many hours of search we found him in the village we had just left. My husband was more and more ill. We had to lift him onto a horse, and it was with great trouble that we reached our next stop. We shortened our coverage more and more in order to reduce chances of separation. After spending the night beneath the stars, we finally reached a village called Sholokhov. The people there were poor, but we had the chance of meeting a cultured Pole, a bridge and road engineer, who received us with great care and gave us three rooms in his house. We found some food at our host's including chicken and eggs.

This time we were at a relatively short distance from Sochi, where our wandering was, provisionally, to come to an end. Since we were now able to go by road, we needed at any cost a carriage and bench cart. Unfortunately, this need became more difficult to satisfy than we thought. The inhabitants of Sholokhov, understanding nothing of our expedition, assumed at first that we intended to go to Sochi to restore the old regime. Others, taking us for itinerant tradesmen, refused to help us at all.

We spent six days in Sholokhov in calm and rest. As for our host, he was so interested in the teaching of our Master than he abandoned his work to join us.

Before leaving Sholokhov Gurdjieff took us on an extremely interesting excursion. In effect, we were looking for dolmens which were numerous in the region. What surprised me, once I was able to admire certain of them, is that they were located very close to scattered houses in which highlanders had taken residence. One of them, for instance, was converted into a chicken coop.

∽

My memories and my notes end here. A few days later we were in Sochi. The most important stage of our exodus finished thanks to the wisdom, the perspicacity and the incomparable abilities of our Master.

I beg my readers' indulgence. If my account has seemed to them at times disordered, it is because I noted my impressions in haste, during a pause, seated most often on a tree trunk in the midst of a wood.

IN PLACE OF A CONCLUSION

After this account by my mother, it is not my intention to continue incessantly with other numerous adventures and trials which awaited Gurdjieff before recounting the safe conclusion and freedom of movement achieved by the group. On the whole, the trek across the Caucasus might seem long in the eyes of the reader. This may seem so because of frequent turnings about, circumspection and strategic pauses.

After Sochi, and before we arrived at the Prieuré, there was Tbilisi where I was born, Turkey—a country in transformation—Austria, Germany and finally France. The circle of my voyage through time is, so to speak, closed. In the place of a conclusion, I take the liberty to draw the attention of my readers to two brief accounts which have the virtue, at least, of being previously unpublished[12].

MY MOTHER AND HER WISH TO HAVE A CHILD
Her own account of meetings with Rasputin

This episode in my life took place during the second half of World War I, one year before the fall of the tsarist regime. I was very young when the chance came to be in the company of a truly astonishing person who, still today, is the object of many studies and legends. I speak of Rasputin.

It was 1916. The Emperor and Empress of the Russias had seen Rasputin again at the house of the Grand Duchess Militza Nikolaevna. According to rumour, he was blessed with a miraculous gift to cure the ill.

A simple peasant from distant Siberia, he went from village to village caring for sick children with prayer and supernatural powers. Attracted by mysticism and believing in the power of prayer, Tsar Nicholas II was interested in the personality of Rasputin. Everyone knew that the case of Alexis, the crown prince who suffered from haemophilia, was desperate. Rasputin's hour came when he was summoned to court to try to staunch the bleeding of the Tsarevich's nose. Until then, all medical efforts had failed, but Rasputin simply laid his hands on the nose and the bleeding stopped immediately.

One can understand that from that day the imperial family had no other recourse but to call upon Rasputin whenever it was necessary. Rasputin's appearance at court became more and more frequent. Apparently, the imperial couple could not live without the *starets*, or holy man.[13] Since the Tsar's functions were extremely demanding, the Tsarina Alexandra Feodorovna received Rasputin most of the time. The role of the *starets* changed radically. Numerous courtesans began going directly to him. Thus, the simple monk was transformed into a privileged mediator for the petitioners who sought favours and protection of the Tsar.

The hold Rasputin exercised over the courtesans was re-enforced by his prophetic gifts. He had predicted the fate of Russia, his own death and that of the imperial family. More precisely, he had announced to his protectors, 'I will die first, then you shall all follow me'.

Further, his strange powers as a hypnotist explained the undeniable success he had the women of the court. Although neither monk nor priest, Rasputin did not hesitate to pass himself off as a *starets*. Finally, this disturbing person who had become legendary joined my circle of friends.

At this time I lived in Saint Petersburg with my husband, a psychiatrist who spent almost all his time with his practice. I felt terribly alone and dreamed of a child to fill my emptiness. Sensitive to my desire, a patient of my husband's, the wife of the minister Shelkovnikov, invited us to her house to meet Rasputin. She intended to ask him if he could foresee the desired birth of a child.

By mischance I had to leave Saint Petersburg. My husband, however, accepted the invitation and told me later that Rasputin was the star of the evening. The wife of the minister had asked the question which plagued me so much, and Rasputin asked my husband, who has considerably older than I was:

'Is your wife young?'

And, to an affrmative response, he added:

'Bring her to me first, and I will say afterwards what will come about'.

The *starets* had the habit of using the second person singular form for everyone.[14]

A month later, we were invited once more to dinner at the same place. When Rasputin entered the dining room

I saw for the first time this enigmatic figure. He was of medium height, a bit on the heavy side, full-haired with a thin beard. He wore a *kaftan* (a loose Russian tunic) and high boots. His blue-green eyes were especially expressive, particularly when he looked at a young woman. Many attributed to that hypnotic gaze the power of holy men to get what they wanted.

There were ten at the table. My friend placed Rasputin at her right and me at her left. While eating he kept looking at me and talking to me, but he became silent whenever the others stopped talking to listen to what he was saying. I assumed he had chosen me to be his interlocutor because of my youth.

When my friend asked Rasputin if I had a possibility of bearing a child, he answered:

'One, surely'.

In effect, that was to be the case.

After dinner, the guests went into the salon. I sat on a couch and Rasputin sat beside me.

'Do you know,' he said, 'that I have never read a single book to this day?'

This confession did not surprise me. Peasants at that time were almost all illiterate.

One of the guests came up and asked Rasputin rather stupidly if he often went to court. The *starets* ignored the question by turning away toward me.

I had heard that at times he had received up to fifty persons in a single morning. I asked for what motives so many wanted to see him.

'You amuse me!' he exclaimed, 'don't you realize that all those who come to see me have something to ask of me? I try my best to satisfy them whether it is a question of someone placed in high circles or a kitchen girl looking for work'.

Aware that the evening was coming to a close, Rasputin became more and more enterprising. He insisted that I go see him as soon as possible. He wanted a definite answer.

Nonchalantly, he brought his chair close to mine, and suddenly I felt his hand on my thigh. I moved away brusquely with indignation.

'Are you afraid of me, dear?' he asked in a sweet manner.

'Not the least bit', I said, shocked.

'Know that I see and hear perfectly. You have no reason therefore to sit so close to me'.

Despite this light banter, Rasputin insisted nicely. He absolutely expected me to visit. My first reaction was 'No, and no!'

But I recall that all my friends, male and female alike, envied me the privilege of meeting the 'most famous *muzhik*',[15] and implored me to invite him to my house so they could meet him too. This is what I said to him that, though he need not expect my visit, he would be nonetheless welcome at my house.

'Name the day and hour!'

It was Saturday evening. On the following Wednesday, Rasputin had to go to Siberia.

'If it suits you', he said, 'telephone me on Monday. You only have to say that the doctor's wife is calling'.

I rose briskly and asked my hostess to take my place by the *starets* so that I could leave unnoticed. The switch succeeded and I escaped as planned.

On Monday I called Rasputin. I was told that he never comes to the phone, but when I announced 'the doctor's wife,' I heard his voice right away.

'Set the day and the hour when I should come!'

'Wednesday at 3:00 in the afternoon', I said laconically.

The propitious day was not far off. Ten women and two men, including my husband, were at my house. We sat about a big table in the dining room. Precisely at 3:00, several rings sounded at the front door. The porter brought Rasputin to the salon where I joined him right away. He seemed in good humour and greeted me with gallantry. I suggested we take tea in the dining room. But, as soon as I opened the door, his aspect changed. At the sight of my impatient guests, he uttered in an irritated voice:

'Damn, all these good ladies!'

I was pleased seeing him expose himself before everyone in an angry mood. I invited him to sit down, while my guests devoured him with their looks. Each waited for Rasputin to take the lead in talk, but he uttered only a few words as he examined his cup of tea. He took a slice of lemon with his fingers, whose cleanliness left much to be desired.

That very night the *starets* was to leave for Siberia.

'Then, are you coming to wish me bon voyage before I leave?'

'What good would that be? No doubt hundreds will come to see you off'.

He smiled. 'Let it be! For you, I would always have time.'

To my surprise he asked:

'Would a photo of me please you?'

I was trapped.

'The photographer has already sold all his photos of me, but you will receive one very soon. Meanwhile I would like to write a few lines for you to remember me by.'

All the women cried out as one:

'For me too, for me too!'

My husband went to look for writing paper. Rasputin scribbled on the sheets of papers the women handed him. It was obvious that he was concentrating each time he applied the pen. I did not have time to read what he wrote for each of my friends, but I heard many exclamations of surprise and of joy.

As for the inscription meant for me, it was very brief, saying simply:

'Love surpasses mountains, Grigori'. (Grigori Novikh was his real name. He got the nickname *Rasputin* because of his dissolute morals. *Rasputin* derives from *rasputstvo* 'debauched, lustful'; *rasputnik* 'libertine'; Rasputin merited his nickname.)

The writing was in all respects like the scribble of illiterate peasants.

At his departure, Rasputin went about before each of my friends. I do not know what he murmured in their ears, but I saw one after the other jerk away with indignation. Despite the brouhaha, Rasputin approached my great aunt who had recently divorced and remarried:

'And so you've made a new nest my beauty', he said. 'Are you sure you won't abandon a nest a second time?'

I must note here that he had never seen my grand aunt before. Then he went up to another guest—the young wife of a doctor—and looked intently at her as he said:

'You won't find happiness in leading a double life'. In fact, the young woman was sleeping with both her husband and her father-in-law.

Finally, we went with the *starets* to the front door, and we heard from the servants that two armed police were stationed in front of the house during his visit. Rasputin seems to have been well protected.

One day during the icy winter I bumped into him on the street for the last time. He was going by in his sleigh drawn by two horses. I was coming out of a chapel where I had prayed long for a very young friend in critical condition. Rasputin stopped his team and **invited me to get in**, saying:

'I'm going home'.

I explained that I was going to visit a dying friend, but he interrupted me.

'Don't worry about her. Your friend will recover'.

He had already made place for me on his sleigh when I

noticed a group of fools staring curiosity at the person with whom I spoke. Troubled, I uttered a quick 'goodbye' and left.

Hardly two months later I was shocked to read in the press that Rasputin was dead. The whole city, my dear Saint Petersburg, spoke of it for some time. Writing on the subject continues to this day.

THE LAST DAYS OF KATHERINE MANSFIELD

In order to close properly my chapter on the Prieuré, recounted in my memoirs, I think it good to complete it with a charming account by Adele Kafian, written in Russian, which I add here. Remember that Gurdjieff had designated Adele as a medical aid and helper in the service of Katherine Mansfield.

Articles on Katherine Mansfield which appeared in the French newspapers showed me that very few people know how she spent the last part of her life at Fontainebleau-Avon, at the Prieuré. Fate allowed me to be with her up to the time of her death.

Although not a woman of letters, I have been haunted by the idea that it is the duty of everyone who has been brought, if only accidentally, into close contact with great people who have gone from us forever, to relate all that they know to those who love them and are interested in them.

I lived at the Prieuré amongst a group of people considered 'absurd, fervent theosophists' (at least this is what could be read in newspapers at the time). What was the truth of this? Well, the people I saw did not spare their strength in sincere search of the truth. Others tried perhaps to understand God, fixated on an objective ideal. There were those who strived to rid themselves of their faults in pursuit of harmonious development of moral and physical personality. There were also those who simply lived without troubling themselves about complex ideologies.

In effect, to the Prieuré went those who did not find satisfaction in the old ways and means of achievement then current in Europe. The ordinary human spirit demands classification, a label—people do not like unnamed things; that is why the group we formed was stamped with the name 'theosophists'. I do not know if such were there. Our master Gurdjieff did not consider himself one, and was even angered whenever hearing the term used as such. As far as I was concerned, I was a Catholic and have remained one, but am endeavouring to live as a Christian.

With Katherine Mansfield it was never a matter of engaging in lofty spiritual topics. At the time, I did not speak a word of English, and we communicated in rudimentary French. What she sought at the Prieuré I do not know; perhaps everything! She once said to me:

'I like to see how much all the people here work, even doing what they have never done in their lives before, and doing it quite well at that. When I feel better, I shall do my turn of work, and shall write a lot of stories. I already have in mind the subjects I shall treat'.

Personally, I had to make a great effort to join the group at the Prieuré. As a young woman just starting life, I was certain of the infinite possibilities of the human being. I was gifted with an aptitude for drawing, music and singing, but especially with an abundance of untried strength. An endless file of people from all parts of the world, interested in the work done here taught by Gurdjieff, passed through the Prieuré: a sick English woman—an authoress—also arrived here. When I first looked into her large intelligent eyes, I was inwardly drawn to her. Servants were not allowed in this strange house. The residents were expected to do everything themselves. Therefore, I was detailed by Gurdjieff to care for the sick woman. Although I was often uncertain what might give pleasure to this woman with such modest needs, it was a task I accepted with joy.

℘

After a short stay she went away. Katherine Mansfield was ill to such an extent that we did not think we would see her again among us. However, she did return, and seemingly to stay. On Gurdjieff's instructions, a special balcony was constructed for her in the cowshed. There she was to rest and have her strength renewed, perhaps through the radiation of animal magnetism, perhaps by the healthy smell of fresh manure.

It was a tiny balcony, artistically designed, with a small staircase of five or six steps, surrounded by a balustrade comprised of Oriental features. The floor was covered with mats and authentic small Oriental rugs. Gaily decorated cushions and poufs invited relaxing and gazing at the ceiling, cleverly painted by Alexander de Salzmann, our talented artist. On this mural were all kinds of birds, insects and little animals playing hide-and-go-seek among translucent branches. Among this charming profusion could be detected caricatures of all the Prieuré residents. Under the balcony stood our three cows and the mule Dralfit.

When my turn came to work for a week in the cowshed, I gave special care to the little balcony. I decorated the staircase with leaves and branches, after which I sat and awaited the arrival of Mrs Murry (we used to call Katherine Mansfield by her married name). Looking very serious, she would walk up the stairs slowly, carrying a notebook. I began milking the cow and, as ordered, would bring her a glass of fresh milk. I have no idea whether she liked this sort of drink or whether she forced herself to drink it. Nonetheless, she brought it to her lips, saying how amusing it was to listen to the sound of the flowing milk, and that she was able to judge by the sound my fatigue and state of mind. She realised that though I was not accustomed to manual labour, no easy tasks were given to me. Thus a certain warmth in our relationship developed, which meant a great deal to me being away from home for the first time.

Then came Christmas. We all gathered around a huge illuminated Christmas tree. There were many children in the house, for some of the residents had families. Mrs Murry made an appearance in the salon, looking very attractive in a dark purple taffeta dress which was embroidered with tiny flowers and simply cut with shoulder straps like those worn by young girls. Her short hair was smoothly combed over her high forehead. Mrs Murry watched the children receive their presents with great interest. Afterwards she recited some character-scenes in an English dialect. Although I did not understand a word, I followed attentively her mimicry of peasants quarrelling among themselves. The whole company surrounded Mrs Murray, and the children exploded with laughter at her various facial expressions and the sound of her amusing elocutions.

Seeing that Katherine Mansfield was about to leave, I went into her room quickly, put some logs on the fire I had started earlier, and lit the candles on a small bushy Christmas-tree I had dug up in our wood and set before the fire while the party was at its height in the salon.

This is our little tree, just for the two of us, I thought, and nobody else shall see it. It was unadorned but for the candles: one for Mrs Murry, another for myself, and a third for the one for whom she awaits so excitedly. Hearing her footsteps, I stood aside. She opened the door and cried out in surprise. On seeing me she said, 'Adele, why three?'

I told her my little secret, she smiled sadly and sank into the armchair. I covered her shoulders with a long fluffy shawl in wide blue and white stripes. (I could not imagine then that this shawl would later warm me too.) I moved up a footstool, and placing myself near her on the floor, embraced her slim knees. We both sat in silence looking at our Christmas-tree. One candle burnt badly; it flickered and began to go out.

'That's me', she whispered.

I immediately jumped up and blew out the other two, as if to say, 'No, no!'

Alas, this was her last Christmas-tree. I did not know then the superstition about the three candles. I opened her bed, placed a hot-water bottle in it, and bade her goodnight. She did not like being helped to undress.

Shortly after Christmas Mrs Murry received news of her husband: that he was coming to see her. This message cheered her up, and it seemed as if she was feeling better. I saw her write some notes and letters, after which she waited impatiently for the day agreed upon.

Aware that she was suffering from very advanced tuberculosis, I was so glad for her and was hoping for some miracle recovery.

I did not witness her meeting with her husband. I was then very busy in the kitchen. From time to time I had to run to Mrs Murry's room to tidy up, to bring her water and other things. It was a pleasure to catch a glimpse, if only from afar, of her frail silhouette with dark hair which tended to cover her thin shoulders.

She intended to have her husband see all the peculiarities of our house: the theatre, the study-house (built and decorated by ourselves, the steam bath excavated in the slope, the vegetable gardens, the flowerbeds. She wanted to acquaint him with numerous things of interest which aimed at harmonious development. For example, rhythmic exercises, based on the regular movements of Eastern religious dances, were practised. They were performed to the accompaniment of low sounds of music, improvised in our presence. We were advised to do exercises for the development of our critical sense, concentration, discernment, and memory. None of these impeded our hard daily manual work. As for Mrs Murry, perceptive observer, everything interested her, and she wanted to share her impressions with her husband, but it was too late.

In the evening after dinner, Katherine Mansfield and her husband listened to some music in the salon, and afterwards, going upstairs to her room, she seemed to forget all caution and ran up quickly, without even touching the banister, as a healthy person might do. He followed her. She had hardly entered her room when blood began spurting from her mouth. Her husband ran for the resident doctor. He passed me in the corridor as I was taking hot water to them. When I entered the ill woman's room, and saw her sitting on the edge of her bed covering her mouth with her hands as blood gushed through her fingers, I hastened to her with a towel. Gasping for breath, she called for her husband and stared at the door with eyes wide with terror. I ran out and met him in the corridor hurrying with Dr de Stjernvall. I desired greatly to return but threw myself on my bed and wept instead.

For the first time I saw death closely. It took from me the earthly form of the wonderful Mrs Murry, who had brought me beauty and had made easier the hard life of trials I had chosen for myself.

Mr Murry came to me after the funeral, and told me very kindly that his wife had written about me, that he knew how attached I was to her. He asked me to accept and wear her dresses, including her beautiful Christmas gown.

It would have been disrespectful to refuse this kindness. As I was carrying her clothes to the wardrobe along the top red corridor, which once led to monks' cells (the house was converted from an old monastery), a little red-breasted bird flew in through the window, circled over me and fluttered out again. I remembered my grandmother's tales in which the souls of the departed took on the shape of birds to visit close ones. I started to pray for the peace of her soul.

Before leaving, Mr Murry came to say good-bye. Then, opening a small box, he took out a ring encrusted with rubies. He explained that Mrs Murray had received it from him on their betrothal, and that it was her favourite ring. He insisted that I should take it, adding that doing so would surely have given pleasure to his wife. I wore this ring on special occasions; to me it was a symbol: Katherine Mansfield had scattered over the entire world a garland of bright, beautiful stories. Her love knew no bounds. She grieved for every lost soul. She could not and did not want to measure, to calculate. She did not fade away slowly, but her life burned out in a quick bright flame.

Her modest gravestone bears no cross, but her whole being was filled with love, and, carried away by her example, I learned to love mankind.

On the anniversary of her death, Mr Murry came from England, and we went together to the grave to pay her homage. Then I handed back to him the favourite ring of his departed wife.

NOTES

1. For reasons for brevity and to accord with Russian custom, I designate Gurdjieff henceforth by his first name and patronymic, Georgivanich, or simply G.I. (NdS) The French edition provides Gurdjieff's first name and patronymic as Georges Ivanovitch, and although we considered using Georgi Ivanovich for this English edition, the author appreciated the translator's suggestion of using Georgivanich, which better conveys the pronunciation. (LSN)
2. A term invented by Gurdjieff which designates an affected, inappropriate and conceited manner. (NdS)
3. The name which I used for Dr Leonid de Stjernvall until his death in 1938. (NdS)
4. Maurice Leblanc. (PBT)
5. Historically known as Saint-Aubin-jouxte-Boulleng. (NdS)
6. Russian hors d'oeuvres. (LSN)
7. The term used for doctors' wives, according to Russian uses, which G.I. used each time he addressed my mother. (NdS)
8. Translation: 'To serve the salad separately or after the main course is a culinary stupidity which marks conventional French cuisine.' (NdS)
9. The author's reference to this expression seems to be *Vers l'éveil à soi-même*, the French title of Jean Vaysse's *Toward Awakening*. (LSN)
10. The son of Gurdjieff's sister Anna. (PBT)
11. People from Imereti, Georgia. (LSN)
12. The author means that these accounts were previously unpublished *in French*. In this English edition of the author's work, we would like to acknowledge that a different translation of Adele Kafian's piece on Katherine Mansfield was published in the October 1946 issue of *The Adelphi*. (LSN)
13. A *starets* is considered a prophet in pre-Bolshevik Russia. (NdS)
14. Before the Bolshevik revolution, the second person plural pronoun in Russian was used to address everyone outside of one's intimate circle of friends. (PBT)
15. *Muzhik* is the common term for a serf or peasant on an estate. (PBT)

PHOTOGRAPHS

Jeanne de Salzmann with, left to right, Natalie de Salzmann, Nikolai de Stjernvall, Leonid Savitsky and Yvonne Pinder.

Michel de Salzmann and Nikolai de Stjernvall at the Prieuré, 1929 or 1930.

Left to right: Valentin Anastasieff, Tom Peters, Luba Gurdjieff, André Lapina, Anatole Mercurov and Fritz Peters.

Automobile excursion in the twenties—Bernard Metz, one of the first inhabitants of the Prieuré, and Leonid de Stjernvall.

Dr de Stjernvall, Julia Ostrovksy, and Gurdjieff's sister Sophia.

Nikolai de Stjernvall, Michel de Salzmann and Leonid de Stjernvall, New York City, January 1931.

Sotteville, Normandy, Nikolai de Stjernvall above, left to right, Elizaveta de Stjernvall, Irene Lapina and Leonid de Stjernvall. In front, their dog Nora.

Nikolai de Stjernvall on the bicycle, left to right, Adele Kafian's son Pierre, Eve Taylor, daughter of Gurdjieff, and her brother Paul Taylor.

Left to right, Dr de Stjernvall, Nikolai de Stjernvall, Svechnikov and his daughter in Normandy in the 1930s.

www.ingramcontent.com/pod-product-compliance
Lightning Source LLC
Chambersburg PA
CBHW062114280426
43661CB00111B/1432/J